Healing For Life

Also by Clare Nonhebel

FICTION

Cold Showers

The Partisan

Incentives

Child's Play (Lion, 1998)

**Eldred Jones, Lulubelle and
the Most High** (Lion, 1998)

NON-FICTION

Healed and Souled
(by Ashuli: co-written with Joseph Stefanazzi)

Don't Ask Me to Believe (Lion, 1998)

Far From Home (Lion, 1999)

To all the people mentioned in this book,
with love.

Healing *For Life*

A remarkable exploration of the successes and failures of spiritual healing

CLARE NONHEBEL

A LION BOOK

Published by
Lion Publishing plc
Sandy Lane West, Oxford, England
www.lion-publishing.co.uk
ISBN 0 7459 5036 1

First edition 2000
10 9 8 7 6 5 4 3 2 1 0

A catalogue record for this book is available
from the British Library

Typeset in 12/14.5 Garamond ITC
Printed and bound by WS Bookwell, Finland

INTRODUCTION

Hi! This is God. I've been wanting to talk to you. I've been waiting for the moment when you'd open this book.

Yes, that's right. No, you haven't misheard.

The God? Of course, *the* God. There is only one, you know.

Why would I want to talk to *you*?

If you don't mind my saying so, that's an odd question, coming from you. I made you, invited you into the world, and I was delighted when you accepted my invitation. I've followed your progress every inch of the way, applauded when you learned to walk or said your first word; grieved with you when you failed to achieve some goal you really wanted; waited patiently when you went off in some strange direction, trying to meet somebody else's goals and forgetting about your real purpose here.

Sorry? What *is* your real purpose here? Yes, I thought you might have forgotten that one. But don't worry. You haven't forgotten really. And you have been listening to me, deep down, all along. But you live in a noisy world. So many distractions. All those voices, inside you and outside, telling you who to be and what you want.

That's why I want to talk to you now.

You've been trying so hard – too hard, perhaps.

You've been learning so much – and some of those

7

things you found you then had to unlearn, because yesterday's wisdom becomes tomorrow's platitude.

You've been achieving, changing, striving, controlling, teaching, loving, hating, fighting, going with the flow, going with the crowd, going without.

Now it's time to be still.

Listen to one voice only, and you'll recognize your own.

You've been looking for me high and low – and quite rightly, because that's exactly where I am. In the highs and in the lows.

I've been here all the time, on the edges of your life, waiting to be invited, to be heard. Now, for a little while, let me be at the centre of your thinking. I'm already at the centre of your being.

Does that sound threatening – like an alien taking over your life? Don't be afraid. It's nothing like that. I never invade your space. Didn't I give you that space inside you, where you could always be alone, think your own thoughts, make up your own mind? I'd never intrude on that. I want you to be you. I'm on your side.

Have I seemed angry with you at times? Have I withheld my approval, failed to give you support in some cherished project? Let somebody you loved leave you when you so much wanted them close to you?

I know. But I have never once been angry with you – never once in your whole life. And I never will be. I love you.

Oh yes, there is an angry side to God. I am angry. So are you. We get angry about the same things, you and me. We get angry about cruelty, waste and injustice.

So why am I cruel to you, wasteful with the precious lives of those you have loved and lost, and unjust in giving some people benefits but forgetting about others – about you?

I'm not out to justify myself. Have you noticed that when someone starts justifying themselves, it goes hand in hand with blaming someone else? So I'm not going to go into involved explanations of why I do things sometimes in ways you don't like.

What I am going to say is I'm not blaming you.

I'll say that again, because I want your heart to hear this, as well as your mind.

I don't blame you.

For anything.

For anything that goes wrong in your life, I don't blame you.

Yes, I know you feel bad, and guilty, and uncomfortable.

I know you've done things you wish you'd been strong enough to resist doing. I know the uneasiness that comes from knowing you've compromised on the truth, or let yourself down – failed to meet your own standards. What I'm saying is – by the time you're aware of this, *it has been dealt with*.

Even while you were still trying – so hard, sometimes! – to argue with yourself and convince yourself you'd done nothing wrong really, your spirit was writhing with pain and crying out to me. And I heard. I always hear. And I deal with the problem instantly. It may take you some time to be aware of this. Your mind struggles to acknowledge that you've grieved yourself. It's a tough one.

Do you know why your prayers don't seem to get answered sometimes?

You are far better at praying than you know.

Think about it again.

Your prayers are far better than you are conscious of.

They are more heartfelt than your heart is aware of.

They are more thorough, more far-sighted, more extravagantly generous, more forgiving, longer-term, wiser, humbler, deeper, in every way than the prayers your mind can form.

Your spirit is constantly praying, constantly talking to me, in ways that your mind is not aware of.

That's not fair?

Yes, it is. You wouldn't want to be limited by your mind, would you? If all that's in your mind is all there is – and all you are – then you would be very limited. And you are not limited. You are made in my image and likeness, and there are no limits to me.

If you know your own mind, are you aware of how limited that knowledge is? How much more there is to you?

Does it worry you, that I know you more deeply than you know yourself? It shouldn't do. How could I protect you, if I didn't see further than you see?

Think of all the things that take up space in your mind every day. All those practical, niggling details that aren't very interesting, or very significant in the great scheme of things, but they're all very necessary.

But is that all your life is? Lists of chores, things to do, projects to achieve, people to contact, people to provide for, people to meet, trains to catch, parties to go to, people to visit, people to care for, appointments to keep, dates to make, targets to reach, money to get, money to spend, money to give, weight to lose?

Is that your life?

No, thank God, it's not.

Deep down, another life is being lived. Your spirit and my Spirit are communicating. You are making choices about the world you live in. You and I are discussing the course your life will take. We are weighing up the options, deciding what's best for you and what's best for the people in your life.

Incidentally, did you know that there's never any conflict of interests? What's *really* good for you is good for everyone. What's *really* best for the other person will be good for you as well. You have evidence to the contrary? I know. Be patient with me. No, I'm not justifying myself. But here's another truth: *You understand me a lot better than you think you do.*

Your spirit understands me, because your spirit is like me. You want the best for yourself. You want the best for your world. You're a nice person really. How could you not be? I made you.

But listen now.

Listen to yourself.

How come your mind is so often unaware of what your spirit is telling me?

Why are you in such conflict with yourself that I – even I, God – can't answer all of your prayers, simply because they contradict one another so much?

No, you tell me the answer to that one.

'Lord, make my mother well. Don't let her die.

Lord, make that person love me. Don't let her/him get away and go and love someone else.

Lord, I hate my job.

Lord, I want more money.

Lord, where are you? Why don't you hear me? Why don't you stop the suffering in the world?'

But I'm here. I'm here. I'm here, with your spirit. You and me.

You and I, we are listening to your mind. We can hear your distress – and it's real, and it's significant, and you must never overlook it or make light of it. But your mind isn't listening to us – to the deep-down self that is the real you, backed up by me, the one who is always on the side of the real you. You and me against the world.

Why 'against the world'? Because the world is so often against the real you. The world convinces you that the world is all there is: that it's the end of the world if somebody dies, or prefers to be with someone other than you, or if people aren't nice, or everyone seems to have more than you – more fun, more life, even *more God*.

As if it wasn't enough for you to have to put up with painful situations in your life – and they are really and truly painful, not imaginary grievances or futile self-pity – the world turns the knife in the wound by telling you: *This is you! This is all there is to you! This is all there is to life! And you blew it!*

Cruel. Yes. Unjust, untrue, callous, and wasteful.

That's why I'm not on the side of the world, even though I made it. I only made it for you. If it turns against you, it's not fulfilling the task I asked it to do.

But here's the good news. I never turn against you.

I'm going to say it one more time now – and this time, you'll know. You'll say, 'Oh, that's obvious! That's old stuff. I always knew *that*!'

See how quickly you learn?

But I'll say it anyway, just for revision purposes.

I don't blame you.
For anything.
Got it?
Good.
Now we can talk.

1

Hi! This is Clare Nonhebel.

No, not God. Not the author of being. Just an author. Just me. Sorry.

On the other hand – why apologize to you?

Do you apologize for being just you, for not being God?

I hope not. I can talk to God any time, anyway. This is probably my first opportunity to talk to you.

What is your view about God talking to people, personally, individually, in just the same way that another human being would talk to you?

Some people would say that anyone who claims to hear God speak to them is mentally unstable. Others would say it could only really happen to a special person, one with unusual perception and wisdom maybe, or someone especially holy.

I don't fall into those categories, and anyway we don't need them.

For God to decide to talk to you, you must have one characteristic only: to be one of his people. One of his family.

And who are they?

Well, everyone. Everyone created by the creator of all human beings. No exceptions. No, not even 'self-made men'! (Who are they kidding?)

God has always spoken to people. There is absolutely nothing new about it. Jewish history recounts innumerable communications from God directly to his people – via Abraham, Moses, Isaac, Jacob, David, Elijah. Christian history continues the pattern – via Matthew, Mark, Luke, John, Mary, Peter, Paul.

Ah, but relatively very few! And all unusual people – people already highly committed to God. They were hardly – if it's not rude to say so – normal people. Not your average man or woman in the street.

But they may have been very ordinary to start with. And to start with, there were only a few called, certainly. But perhaps these were stepping-stones, to show everyone else that they too have the potential to be chosen, to grow special, to become holy, and to go beyond the limits of ordinary human capability.

God started small, in calling and choosing his team, which is probably the way that suits us because we all started small. (Though to hear some people talk about themselves, you do wonder, don't you?)

One sperm, one egg, one act of fusion. The same beginning for us all. (Ah, but the really important people came from a *super-sperm* and a *really superior egg* and the meeting was second only to the collision of Mars and Venus! And who do *they* think they're kidding?)

So, if God wants to talk to us all – what does he want to talk about? Himself? Us?

We're not going to find out unless we're prepared to take the risk that he might raise some topics in our minds that we're trying hard to avoid.

My own experience of discussions with our creator is that he has a habit of making straight for the Keep Out signs.

In a way, I find that reassuring. If I was listening to myself, I wouldn't do that. I know exactly which topics I'd like to avoid. So listening to God is not the same as listening to my own imagination.

I can also hear answers to questions which are not the answers I expected.

I have certainly heard advice which is very far from anything I wanted or hoped to hear.

There is a price to pay for listening to God. Once I ask to hear his voice clearly, I may find it hard to pretend I don't know what he wants me to do with my life. I can always ignore him, of course. But I'll know that I'm doing that.

It may seem easier not to listen to him in the first place.

Except... there are times in most people's lives when they can't help it; when some unwelcome idea nags away at them; when they find themselves prompted to do something good that will cause them embarrassment or inconvenience.

One occasion, for me, came when I was just beginning to have some success as a freelance journalist. It was a hard-won achievement; I had struggled for years with illness, then, finally in better health, had got settled in a job in a public relations agency. Freelance feature writing for magazines was a sideline, but when one magazine offered to buy more of my work if I could write more, I decided to take the risk of leaving the regular job and writing full-time.

It's an oversubscribed market, but I was just beginning to make headway and my file of published articles was growing nicely, when the time for renewing my union membership fell due.

I was filling in the form when something stopped me. A call to prayer? I'm not sure what you'd call it. My attention was drawn to the copy of the union newsletter I'd just received. On the front page was a rather malicious item: photos of journalists who had continued working during a strike, with *Scabs!* printed in large letters across their pictures. The paper gave their names and called for members to blacklist them and never work with them again.

I didn't like it. The cause for striking was not a serious issue of workers' rights, and the arguments for it sounded petulant. Freelance work is a precarious way to earn a living, and if some freelancers decided to support their families rather than support the strikers, I felt they had every right to make that decision.

I went back to filling in the form, and got stopped again. It was one of those odd moments when you feel a presence of God. But why now? Here?

A distinct, gentle voice in my ear said, 'If you don't like the organization, don't be a member of it any more.'

I ignored it. Freelancers need support, and membership of a union is a badge of professionalism – a sign that you're serious about it. It was printed on my letterhead. I might not get so much work without it.

But every time I went to complete the form for renewal of membership, the thought returned: *Don't be part of something you don't agree with.*

So I tore up the form and threw it away, along with the newsletter.

I needn't have worried about the effect on my work. It was only a few weeks later that it became clear that God wanted me to do another kind of work from now on, praying for healing with people who were troubled or sick.

It was not a career. There was no salary, no pension, no status. It certainly wasn't something I knew anything about, nor anything I'd planned. But it was a full-time commitment. I certainly didn't have time to be a journalist!

Would it have happened that way if I hadn't listened to that prompting in my spirit and thrown away the union card? I don't know. I suspect it wouldn't; that it was one of those turning points when you have to decide whether to do things your way – which is logical and sensible – or to go with what God seems to be asking of you.

Having grasped the idea that God wanted me to pray with people for healing, I now had to do a lot more listening. His idea of healing was not at all like mine. I had no experience, and everything to learn.

I'd said yes to whatever he wanted me to do. I didn't have much doubt that his way must be better than any plan I might come up with for my own life. I just didn't feel able or qualified or suitable or even inclined to do it. And I really didn't know what healing – God's method – was all about. Why did he need me at all? Why not just heal people directly, one to one? Or at least pick someone who actively wanted to do this kind of work and had asked for it?

I had kind of asked for it: that is, the thought had flashed through my mind, 'That's a good thing to do; it must be nice to help people like that.' But it wasn't a prayer, or not a conscious one. I hadn't thought any more about it. I was surprised God would listen to such a fleeting thought, and more surprised that he'd take it seriously.

I needed him now to talk to me, at length and in

great detail. I wanted it all spelled out before I started. But that wasn't his way of working. When I prayed, I got small doses of information, as the need arose. I was learning step by step, when I wanted to have the complete instruction manual in my hands before I said a word to anyone.

My main worry was that all the healing ministers I'd heard of ended up in places like Wembley Stadium, shouting into microphones and commanding disabled people to leap out of their wheelchairs and run the marathon. It was not my cup of tea. I'm not an extrovert, and physical stamina is not my strong point either. Standing up in front of crowds doing anything at all sounded to me like a nightmare, even before being called a crank and phoney and all kinds of other names.

Still, he was God and I wasn't. After several sleepless nights, I ended up in the kitchen at three in the morning, and gave in gracefully.

'OK, Lord, I'll do it. If you want me to do healing rallies in Wembley Stadium, I will. Just, could you make sure I don't faint with fright or anything?'

I heard a distinct chuckle, then an amused voice saying, 'But Clare, you'd hate it!'

I was astonished. 'Of course I'd hate it! What's that got to do with anything?'

'I'm your Father. I know what you like. If I want you to do something, I'll give you a way that suits you.'

Obvious, when you think about it. Only, I hadn't thought about it like that. I thought God commanded and we obeyed. No questions allowed.

My idea of God underwent a rapid change.

'You mean, you won't ask me to do *anything* I don't like?'

'Not quite. It means if I ask you to do something, and you say yes, then my purpose will be achieved. But I have a million ways of achieving that purpose, not just one. I choose a way that's suitable for you. I made you to be you, not someone else.'

'But do you have a preferred choice? I mean, would it be more effective if I psyched myself up to do public healing rallies, rather than cowering in the kitchen asking you to do it some way I can cope with?'

I still wasn't getting the hang of this. In my childhood, the parent said what had to be done, and the children did it. I kind of expected the same system to operate with God and his children.

'I offer you the easiest choice first,' was the answer I heard. 'Easiest and most effective for you in the long run. But if you can't face it, and you still want to say yes to me, come back and discuss it. There are always other options.'

'But why would I turn down the easiest?' I said. 'If the one you offer me first is the easiest, I wouldn't be likely to choose a harder one, would I?'

'People do,' he said. 'They choose something that feels easier at the time. It may not be, in the long run. But they do have that choice.'

'Oh.' I took a while digesting this, then said, 'I think I'll have your first choice for me. You want me to heal people, but not be a healer doing big public services? What do I do then?'

'I'll send people to you. The ones I'll send you will need to be healed in the same way that you were healed yourself: that is, they will be people who are already healing many other people and are not aware of it. So their healing may not show instant results, because they are going to have to go at the pace of all those people who are relying on them for their own health.'

That made sense to me. Different people have different ways of being healed. Mine had included other people. I had not got sick on my own and I knew, even at the time, I would not get healed on my own. I had to stay where I was, in my own neighbourhood. Only when I had refused to go into hospital, or to Lourdes, or to Harley Street, had I been healed. At home. And I could see it had had an effect on people around me. In a way, they had also got healed, sometimes of things they hadn't known were troubling them.

So I could see that if God sent people to me, he would pick the ones who needed to be healed in that way too. Privately, at home, carrying on with their own lives, and affecting all the people around them, who were also sick and in need but might not know it.

A few people started to arrive, and brought others. Then I was invited to give a talk to a small group. From there, I was invited to go and pray with the members of a prayer group that had run into difficulties – arguments, gossip, work-worship, and religious politics.

And it was there, one evening, that my next instruction arrived.

It was a real bombshell to me.

He asked me if I was still willing to do as he chose. I said I was.

He said, 'Will you fail for me?'

2

I may have been slow on the uptake, but I couldn't see the point of praying with people in order to fail to heal them. What good would it do them to be disappointed? What would it do to their faith in God? And – let's not be polite here, Lord – what was it going to do to me?

He was not deterred. 'There are people in this prayer group whom I have asked, on many occasions, to pray with sick people, and they've refused because they're afraid of failure. They're afraid to start, in case they don't get results and look stupid.'

'So you want me to pray with people for them to be healed, and then when they don't get healed, those other people will be delighted because someone else got egg on her face instead of them?'

'Something like that.' Again, the voice sounded amused.

'Well, thanks a bunch. Who needs a gift like that, Lord? Not me! Pick some other mug!'

'I have,' he said sadly. 'But they won't do it.'

Suddenly, it didn't seem like a joke.

'Seriously,' I prayed, 'seriously God – the real one, my Father in heaven, the Father of Jesus Christ, and I don't want to hear anyone or anything else – are you seriously asking me to pray with people and fail?'

'No. You can't fail, with me. I'm not setting you up for ridicule. You will never be shamed or disgraced. I don't play games. I love you. I love them. But yes, you will fail to get the results they expect and want, and yes, they will see that as your failure. They will laugh at you and call you names. But they will also lose their fear of failing, because I will show them – finally, when they listen to me – that when you do what I ask of you, you can't fail me.'

'So, OK. Let me get this straight, though. Someone asks me to pray for their sickness to be healed, and I agree to pray, and they get worse.'

'No. No one will be hurt. No one will get sicker. No one will stay sick. I said, with me you can't fail. But it will be seen as failure. You will be blamed. This is what you will do for me.'

'Abba, what is the point of praying, if there are to be no results?'

'There will be results. But they are not your business. I'm asking you to do the praying and leave the results to me.'

I was on a course, a year later, run by a local church – a kind of spiritual refresher course. As part of it, we got into groups and talked about ourselves, including the work we did or the way we spent our time. I said that I spent most days praying with people who were not well or who were in trouble.

Later on in the course, each member had a one-to-one discussion with their group leader. When it came to my turn, the lady leading the group said, 'I've been wanting to ask you about your healing ministry. Have you... has the Lord *blessed* your ministry?'

Neat, huh? Much more diplomatic than, 'How many

miracles have you got under your belt? Do let's hear some miracle stories!'

'Yes,' I told her. 'He has.'

She waited. I waited. After a long pause, she went on to another subject. I wasn't being deliberately difficult, but there didn't seem to be any words to explain, and I didn't think she'd be too thrilled to hear about all the failures the Lord had blessed me with.

I'm not so sure now. It's sixteen years after some of those 'failed miracles' and they've taken on a different perspective. With hindsight, it seems to me now that the Lord did something amazing for each of those people who didn't get what they asked for originally. What happened in some cases was this: they got close to getting what they wanted, and at the moment when they could see it ahead of them, they made a choice.

Some said yes.

Some changed their minds and said no.

Some seemed to let the choice be made for them, by people around them or by circumstances, and events unrolled so that only one choice was left to them finally.

At the time, I couldn't accept it. Why would anyone refuse to be healed? And whatever the reason, how could God allow it?

Some of the people who were not healed, or saw their loved ones stay ill or die, got angry with God. Most of them got angry with me.

But none of them got angry with themselves.

Why not?

I guessed because God didn't want it. He didn't blame them. He didn't want them to blame themselves. He didn't want them to blame me either. He said if they could forgive me, they would still be healed, in their spirit. He didn't blame himself. And he didn't want them to blame him, but it would be better than blaming either themselves or someone else, because blaming him would be a shortcut to the truth. Everyone, he said, knew him, at their deepest level. Everyone knew he was good.

To rage against circumstances, self, and other people was not constructive. To rage against God at least brought them back into contact with him, and he would use that contact for good.

He had given them free choice – a sacred gift. If they used it, they were doing something sacred – using a gift given by God. That in itself was contact with God.

If they chose not to be healed, they had the right to make that choice.

It was only when they claimed to have no choice, and said they had been tricked or manipulated, or others had made them make some choice, or life had left them no choice, or God had given them no choice, that they went off course. They parted company with God, because they parted company with reality.

The reality was that everyone had free will, and made their own choices – even when they chose to see themselves as victims, and abdicated their choice in favour of letting themselves be swept along, like swimmers floating in a strong current, instead of choosing to swim either with it or against it.

No one could live without constantly making choices. And whatever their choice, God would accept it. Uncritically. He would not protect anyone from the consequences of their choice because, if he did, it wouldn't really be free choice. A person wouldn't really be free to experience life, if God made everything have the same outcome no matter which choice they made.

This really didn't meet my theology.

It made no more sense to me than God saying to me, in the middle of the night in the kitchen, 'But Clare, you'd hate it! Why would I ask you to do something you'd hate?'

Why would God ask people to accept a miracle and be healed, if they felt, when the moment came, that they couldn't face it?

I wanted to know reasons. I couldn't imagine a reason why anyone wouldn't want to be healed of an infirmity. Surely it's horrible being sick? And if people had reasons for wanting to keep their illness, surely those reasons couldn't be good ones, so why would God allow it?

I had a lot to learn, and I still have more questions than answers. But I have changed the questions, over the years.

I no longer ask whether God can really heal people. I have seen people healed, including from conditions that were not responding to any of the conventional or unconventional medical cures. I have seen miracles. And I have seen failures. I am sure God can heal, and always wants to.

I am just no longer sure about the difference between God's failures and God's successes. I am beginning to believe what he said at the beginning – that he cannot fail; that even his failures are successes, and that he has a million ways of achieving his success stories, whereas we see success in terms of whether we get what we want or not.

Is healing always the best thing for people?

Do people sometimes have good reasons for not wanting physical healing?

And can God ever really be served by failure? My failure?

Let's take a look at some of the people who said no. That way, you can ask your own questions. Maybe you'll arrive at some different answers. If so, I hope you'll let me know.

3

I heard about Alicia from someone in the church, who was asking for prayers for her. She was a little girl with cancer, and her parents were desperately anxious. She had just had treatment, which had been successful, but there was always the chance the disease would crop up again somewhere else.

As I was praying for her, it seemed that something could be done for her, so I asked the priest if he thought the parents would like the child to be prayed with, in the prayer group I attended. The parents accepted.

In the days before the group met, I prayed a lot for the child, and a picture began to emerge of a little girl who was close to God and needed a lot of peace. It seemed it would be hard for her to keep her balance in a very busy world, with lots of rush and anxiety, and she would need times of calm.

This wasn't really unusual. Parents provide so many sources of activity and stimulation for their children, and lead such busy lives themselves, that children are often deprived of peace – winding-down time, freewheeling time, nothing time. Our society has become afraid to be bored, even for a minute. People are creative in finding ways to occupy their time, but peace sometimes gets sacrificed.

So it seemed clear to me that when Alicia arrived, the best way to pray would be to ask the group to pray with her for peace.

The group met, and the priest chose a few of us to lay hands on the child. The others would sit round, pray and sing.

The parents arrived – without the child.

'Where is she?' the priest asked them.

She wasn't coming, they said.

'Was she frightened of the idea of coming into a group to be prayed with?' he asked them.

No, she had liked the idea, they said. But they had had a busy day, visiting people, and by the evening she was tired, so they had sent her to bed.

I asked them if they would like to set another date for their daughter to come and be prayed with. They said no; they would have the prayer themselves, if that was all right.

We prayed with the parents, but it was hard. There seemed to be a mental block of some kind. The atmosphere was heavy around them. If our only way to reach the child was through them, she wouldn't be easy to reach.

After some time, the weight in their minds seemed to be lifting. It felt different. I had a word with one of the other people praying – an elderly West Indian lady, experienced in prayer. She said she had felt the same thing in them – a solid mental block, like concrete in the brain, but gradually had felt it dissolve. She felt we had done all we could, as far as the parents were concerned. It was a pity, she said, that they had not brought the child.

We asked the couple how they felt, and they said they felt good – peaceful. I told them the child needed a lot of peace – not too much excitement – and that although her condition was apparently stable after her medical treatment, she was very tired. Even if she clamoured to do things, the best thing the family could do for her was to keep life quiet – even boring!

They agreed. There would be no problem with this, they said.

One of the priests who knew the family and had come along to the group with them rushed forward. He could get them a place on a pilgrimage to Lourdes, he said. The places were actually all booked, but he would personally make sure that places were vacated for them. The whole family would be on the plane next week.

The parents thanked him and said it was very kind; the husband would ask for time off work and they would take the other children out of school.

I tried to say that the child needed peace and quiet, and that if all these arrangements had to be made, and unmade, perhaps this trip was not really meant to be. It might be better to stay at home and keep the air of peace we had prayed for this evening.

The following week, the family went to Lourdes. There were services and processions and outings arranged, but after the journey the child became so tired that she could go on none of them, and slept nearly the whole time. The mother became very distressed at seeing her so listless.

A few weeks later, the father phoned. Alicia had pains in her stomach and was crying. The family had been out all day with another family, and the mother was now out for the evening but had left him a list of people to phone to ask to pray if Alicia still felt unwell. I was on the list.

I talked to him again about the child's tiredness –

that she was strong, spiritually, but wouldn't have enough resistance to the disease unless she could have a great deal of peace, and long periods of quiet time on her own or just with the family. Whole day outings were probably a bit beyond her capability at this stage. She needed time to recover from the treatment.

He interrupted me to say that he must get on. There were lots of other people on the list to phone, so he couldn't stay chatting.

A few weeks afterwards, the mother phoned to say that Alicia was very distressed after her first few days back at school. She had a new teacher and seemed anxious about her, although she had always loved school before. I promised to pray, so I went away and asked the Lord to show me what Alicia needed at this stage. Tiredness still seemed to be the major factor. Also, the child was sensitive, and would easily pick up the new teacher's nervousness and tension, and this would make her more tired still.

I phoned the mother back and suggested that Alicia was probably not strong enough yet to go back to school. She was not ill at the moment, but not strong. Her resistance to illness would need to build. Any stress – or even excitement – would drain her.

The mother agreed.

Two weeks later she phoned to say that Alicia couldn't see out of one eye and was very frightened. They had been out for the afternoon to see a film, but couldn't find the one she wanted to see, so they had driven for miles to several other cinemas. By this time, she was crying and tired, so they had given up the idea of seeing the film. She had also had a difficult day at school the day before. She was still going to school every day.

I said I would go and pray, but perhaps the best thing to do for now was put the child straight to bed. Treat it as tiredness, and see if the symptoms would go if she had a sleep.

The mother phoned the next day. They had taken the child straight to hospital after she had phoned me, she said, and had waited there for hours while Alicia was put through a battery of tests. Now they were awaiting the results.

I went and prayed again. I was beginning to have a feeling of sick dread. In the beginning, this hadn't seemed complicated. The child had had cancer but it had responded to treatment. She needed a minor adjustment in her lifestyle, to have the best chance of staying healthy. Everyone has different needs. Alicia's main need was peace. It cost nothing in terms of money or effort, but it seemed to be the one thing the parents were not able to provide for her. The sense of peace they had felt at the prayer meeting seemed to have left them immediately, and was replaced by intense anxiety.

What happened, I asked Alicia's mother, on the occasions when nothing was going on at home? When there was no activity or excitement, did Alicia demand it? Did she become difficult?

No, she said. Quite the opposite. Of all the family, Alicia was quite happy on her own. She could spend hours in her room, playing with her dolls, or just sitting still, daydreaming or thinking. Several adults had remarked on what a peaceful child she was. Other children seemed to calm down when they were with her.

I had one more try. This is who the child is, I told her. This is her nature. Maybe a century ago, it would have been easier, but in today's world it seems unnatural for a child to need peace. It won't automatically be provided for her. You may have to arrange it so there are times for her to be left alone. If she is a source of peace for other people, she will need time to replenish her own.

The mother agreed. But Alicia loved school, and it was surely better for her to lead a normal life – to do all the things other children did. They didn't want her to be left out, and after all, she was well now.

I asked her whether their other children got symptoms when they were overtired; did they have a weak point?

She said yes, one child got sore throats and another ear infections; she herself got migraines and knew it was stress that caused it.

I said that maybe Alicia's weak point was producing tumours. If it could be treated as a sign of stress, like an earache or a sore throat, and she could be given rest, maybe the symptoms would not need to be produced. Prevention was better than cure, surely? A few weeks off school, till she recovered her strength after the last ordeal of tests?

From there, things quickly went downhill. The test results showed growths. They were small, but more tests and an operation were scheduled.

There was silence then, from the family. One phone call, to say Alicia had had an outburst of uncontrolled screaming and crying, wailing in a way that broke their hearts. It was completely out of character for her, they said.

'Tell her to talk to God,' I said. 'Tell her he's listening and he understands and he cares about how she feels.'

The mother phoned back. 'I told her to stop crying and be quiet and say her prayers, but it seemed to make her worse!'

I threw myself at God. 'You've got to help! How can a message like that get so scrambled! They've told the child to shut up and stop making a fuss, instead of telling her you're there with her and you understand her frustration and loneliness!'

The answer was sombre. 'They're doing their best. But they can't give what they haven't got. They don't know I'm there.'

The death of a child is a heartbreak for loving parents, and Alicia's parents loved her. They did everything in their power to make her better. They couldn't have done more.

There was silence from them for a month or so.

Then someone came up to me in the street for a chat, and just before she moved on, said, 'Wasn't it a shame about that child?'

My blood went cold. 'Which one?'

'That little girl whose parents came to the prayer group. She died last month.'

God does not blame parents for doing what they believe is best for their child. He also does not blame either the parents or the child for their reactions to the outcome. He accepts everyone's feelings. I believe he accepted Alicia's parents' resentment towards him that, despite all their agonizing worry and desperate, weary efforts, he did not give them what they asked for: the health of their child.

But I have known many children who have rage and resentment towards their parents because the best that the parents could do for their child just didn't suit the child's needs. God accepts their feelings too. There is no blame, for anyone. He doesn't need to take sides: he's on everyone's side.

When the people involved manage to forgive – God, each other, themselves – it heals them. But forgiveness may be a slow-growing plant; it can't be forced, and anger may need to precede understanding.

This is a process that everyone is engaged in, throughout the whole of our lives – fear, confusion, distress, anger, reluctant forgiveness, then understanding. No sooner have we completed the process over one dilemma, than we start at square one with another one: I've accepted that this tragedy/disappointment might have been used by God for my good, but *this* one? No. Not yet.

About six months after Alicia died, a student for priesthood was visiting our local parish and came to our house.

'This is going to sound a bit strange,' he apologized. 'I was praying in the church and I saw this little girl – not physically, but in spirit. She was about seven years old – bright, determined, quite a strong character. She came up to me and said she knew you and wanted to talk to you. Does this ring any bells?'

'Yes.'

'Oh. Good. Well, she seemed very angry with her parents. All I could think of to say was that I'd pray for her, and I'd tell you.'

'Thanks,' I said. 'Do you normally see people when you pray?'

'It's happened once or twice,' he said. 'I think it's just people letting you know when they need a bit of extra prayer to help them move on.'

That made sense to me. If Alicia had died with unmet needs, anger might prevent her from accepting peace, even when it was made available to her.

A few weeks later, I was praying and fell into a sleep-like state, which is sometimes known as 'resting in the spirit'. It's not a sleep, or a faint, but a sense that all mental and physical function is put on hold, while all your strength is poured into your spirit. Your spirit is alert, but your mind and body are inert. At that time, it happened to me fairly frequently.

A girl came into my view. She was small – and furious. I had never actually met Alicia, but I felt sure it was her. She announced that she was fed up; that her parents wouldn't listen to her and she hated them.

I prayed for some answer that would come from God and not from my own ideas. I didn't know what to say or do for her. The belief among most people I knew was that once someone has died, they are with God and have no further needs from people on earth. When I asked God about this, though, the answer I heard was that we are all on a journey, and continue to make just as much progress after death as before it. At every stage, we are able to both receive help and to give it.

The answer he gave me for Alicia was that she was the parent, not the child. She was bringing up her parents, leading them gently into the truth. That way round, it would work. The other way round, it wouldn't. It was as simple as that.

I told her this, and she nodded thoughtfully. The anger left her. She settled down next to me and appeared to rest, then after a few minutes said, 'I don't really hate them. I think I'll go back to them now.'

'You do that,' I said. 'They'll be glad of your help.'

I fell asleep then and didn't wake up till several hours later, feeling very peaceful.

The physical healing of Alicia had been a total disaster. But Alicia herself was OK: free to be herself and get on with her work.

It could have been done differently, but then the people involved would have had to be different people. As things were, the healing had to take place in the context of their own needs, and in the only way that they could ask for and accept help.

Alicia's need for healing had appeared to be the priority, but, as things turned out, there were other needs for healing in the people around her, and she was stronger than them – strong enough to let everyone make the choices they could cope with.

She was not a sick little girl, helpless and dependent on strong adults for her well-being, but a spiritually steady and patient missionary. Her mission in loving and forgiving the people around her was accomplished. Perhaps her parents had known this when, invited to bring their crisis along to the prayer group, they had left the child at home and brought themselves.

4

By the time the Lord broke the good news to me that he no longer wanted me to have a ministry of failure, I had learned something about detaching myself from the results of prayer.

Prone to self-criticism, I would lie awake at night wondering if I could have prayed more, or with more faith, and whether this would have had more satisfactory results. Because of this tendency, I often forgot to thank God for the more obviously 'successful' results that occurred in the midst of the 'failures'.

A severely handicapped child was due for yet another operation, in addition to the many she had already had in her six years of life. Michelle's body was rigid – like a child carved out of stone – and her legs were stiff and usually either crossed or clamped together. Her carers found it difficult to lift and dress her and change her nappies. It was even more difficult to cuddle her: it was like holding a statue. She had frequent fits. She found it hard to swallow and would often choke, even on liquids. It took ages to feed her.

A friend brought Michelle round to our house so I could pray with her. During the prayer, I felt that she may have been abused and that a lot of the stiffness was due to fear – shock which had stayed in the system for years.

It also seemed that she needed a bit of ordinary home life. She had lived in a children's home for most of her life.

So, with the consent of the matron and the parents, she began to come to the house one day a week. There was prayer, and a walk round the park, and watching television, and sorting the socks, and playing with the dolls' house – and chocolate mousse, which she loved. And, gradually, she started to unwind. She looked more relaxed. Her limbs unclenched.

One sunny afternoon we were sitting in the garden, on the grass. Michelle was on my lap, facing away from me, and I was playing a game of blowing in her ear then sitting still, then blowing in the other one. After a while, she began to turn her head, anticipating the next move. Then there was a smile. Then a giggle.

The friend who originally brought her to the house was kept busy by her own family, but she came as often as she could, and was happy to see the change in her.

Then one day she came with bad news. The hospital consultant had told the parents it was time to operate on Michelle again. To relax and uncross her legs, he felt the best procedure was to cut the tendons behind the knees. This would make the legs floppy and so make her easier to manoeuvre. It would also mean she would never be able to stand or walk, and she was starting to do a bit of both, and even to bounce up and down, bending her knees – laughing at the same time.

It was time, we thought, to provide some evidence that Michelle was no longer so rigid all the time. We took lots of photos of her – standing, bending her knees, lying on her back waving her legs, sitting on the sofa with her knees doubled up under her chin – and smiling.

Michelle's parents showed the photos to the consultant, who said the child was obviously making progress and the operation was unnecessary.

It must have been several months later, on my return from a holiday, that I heard that while I was away Michelle had been operated on. The parents were not sure why it had been done. The doctor had simply looked at the notes and said that as the child was down for the operation, it might as well be done at this time. There was no benefit in not doing it, he said, as the child would obviously never be able to stand or walk, and it would make her easier to handle. So the tendons in her legs had been cut.

Another instance of 'non-healing' was Daniel. Daniel was a young man in his twenties, wheelchair-bound and with brain damage. Although he was young, he was living in an old people's home. His speech was defective and when it could be understood, the sense of it was often jumbled. He had fits, and black moods of depression that sometimes resulted in violence.

When I began to bring Daniel to our house, the matron told me that his medical assessment was that he was incapable of rational thought, of understanding much of what was said to him, or of making decisions for himself. He could be violent and was thought to have emotional problems, possibly relating to his father's death, but appointments with a psychologist had elicited no response from him. He either would not or could not talk about how he felt. He could stand unaided for a minute or two but could not walk, and he was sometimes incontinent. Attempts to feed himself were usually disastrous, so the staff fed him.

The matron also said she had no objection to people

praying if they wanted to, but wouldn't tolerate anyone forcing their religion on anyone else. I said I wouldn't do that, and she seemed content.

I had first met Daniel when I was walking home with a friend. She suddenly said, 'Someone's fallen out of his wheelchair – quick!' and ran into the road where a young man lay face down, apparently having an epileptic fit.

I caught hold of his hand and prayed, and realized he was not having a fit: he was trying to force himself to have a fit. As we prayed with him, he stopped thrashing about and opened his eyes – but was extremely angry at the interference.

The matron came out and told us not to worry – he did have fits, but he also faked them, to get attention. I asked her if he was depressed. It seemed an excessive way of getting attention, to throw himself out of his wheelchair on to the road. She said curtly that he was fine, called two male nurses to lift him back into his chair, and told him to get back indoors.

A few days later, I was walking up the same road, and he was there in his wheelchair, in the middle of the pavement. There was no way of avoiding him.

'Are you OK?' I said. 'I saw you the other day when you fell out of your wheelchair. Are you all right now?'

He looked away.

'It must be horrible to have fits,' I said.

'It is horrible,' he said indistinctly.

'And you were trying to have one,' I said. 'Does that mean you were feeling depressed?'

He shot me a sudden sharp look – surprisingly sharp for someone considered to have low intelligence – but didn't say anything and looked away again. He started mumbling, half-finished sentences that I couldn't interpret. I wondered if he was pretending to be more muddled than he was, rather as he had pretended to have a fit.

'I don't know if you believe in God,' I said conversationally, 'but I do, and I'm quite happy to pray with anyone if they need help. So if ever you do, let me know. I'll see you around; I only live down the road.'

I was walking away when he flung out a hand and grabbed my arm and said, very slowly and clearly, 'Yes – I – do – need – help!'

'Fine,' I said. 'The next healing service we have in our church, I'll let your matron know and we'll come and fetch you. OK?'

'OK,' he said, then, as I walked on, 'Thanks.'

The next healing service was postponed. I asked the priest if he'd go and see Daniel and talk to him first. He called, but Daniel was out, at the workshop he attended in the daytime.

I saw Daniel in the street a few more times, sometimes being lifted into the van that took him to the workshop. He waved an arm and shouted, each time. The attendant smiled and told me not to worry; he was a noisy boy. It seemed an undignified term to apply to a man in his twenties. Daniel turned his head and snarled at her when she said it. 'Oh, naughty boy!' she said.

He waylaid me in the street again, early one evening when he had come home from the workshop.

'When?' he said succinctly. He had a point. There had been a delay of several weeks since he'd said he wanted help.

'Why don't we just go into the home now and I'll ask if I can take you out for tea?' I suggested.

He pulled a face. 'You can try,' he said sardonically.

That encouraged me. Sarcasm surely required a certain level of intelligence, didn't it?

He followed me into the building. I stopped a nurse. 'Is it OK if I take Daniel out for tea?'

'I don't know,' she said. 'I suppose.'

'Yes, now!' said Daniel, loudly and firmly, and she laughed.

'He seems to want to go!' she said. 'Go on then, Daniel – I'll get your coat.'

'No,' he said, and spun the wheelchair round and propelled himself at speed towards the door.

She laughed again and waved. 'Bye, then. Have a nice time!'

'Shouldn't I give you my address?' I said. 'So you know where he is? And what time should I bring him back?'

When I got outside, I had to run to catch up with Daniel, who was zooming down the street as though escaping from Colditz. I was afraid he'd fall out of the wheelchair again. I was also wondering how to get him into our house, which has a high doorstep, and wondering how to pray with him and how much of what was said to him he could actually understand.

He also seemed to be struck by sudden doubt. He stopped, craned his head round, and said, 'Where are we going? What are you going to do?'

That was clear enough, anyway.

'We're going to my house,' I said. 'For tea, and if you're happy with the idea, I'll pray with you. If you're worried about that, I won't. And if you have any doubts, we'll go back to your home right now.'

'Not worried,' he said firmly, and began pushing the wheels round again. For someone with multiple handicaps and severe brain damage, he seemed to be functioning with remarkable efficiency.

I asked a passing neighbour to give me a hand to get Daniel's wheelchair over the doorstep, and we went in and made tea. Daniel wheeled himself round the kitchen, inspecting everything with great interest. He asked where my husband was, his name, and what job he did. I told him, said he'd meet him later, and asked what kind of work Daniel did.

'Fucking boring,' he said, perfectly clearly.

I sat down and looked at him. 'Do you understand everything that's said to you?' I asked him.

He nodded.

'And can you say everything you want to say, or do the words get stuck sometimes?'

'Well,' he said, turning his head away. He looked embarrassed. Then, as if by invitation, he came out with a long stream of language that meant nothing. In the middle of it, he shot me another of those shrewd looks. Then carried on jabbering.

'Lord,' I prayed silently, 'what's going on?'

'Talk to him however comes naturally,' was the answer I got.

I looked at Daniel's face, and couldn't see him except as a person of high intelligence, a sharp mind and strong personality, frustrated by the limitations imposed by disability – and perhaps by the view of him held by others. Had he worked out that it was in his interests to be the poor brain-damaged 'naughty boy'? Did that get him more needed attention than being shrewd and intelligent? Did it make him more lovable, more popular with the people looking after him? Gave him a chance to listen to conversations he wasn't meant to understand?

Talk to him however comes naturally.

'I'm just wondering,' I said casually, 'whether the reason you talk bullshit is because the people around you talk bullshit to you.'

He stopped in mid-babble, grabbed hold of my arm, pulled me towards him and glared into my face. 'I – do – not – talk – bull – shit!' he said furiously.

'Well, you've certainly stopped now,' I agreed. 'So can we talk about why you're so depressed you chuck yourself into the road and try to have fits? Because that sounds to me like suicide.'

He took his time. Several times he began sentences, then stared into space and began mumbling.

I repeated after him the words he had said already, and asked what came next. One or two words at a time, he completed the sentences. He seemed tense and very afraid of what he was saying. Finally, he asked me if I believed in God. I said yes. He said he did as well.

It was another two visits before he told me his father had died. That they had put him in a coffin, and into a grave. For three days, he felt that he himself had died – that he had died with him. He kept saying, 'It was so cold. It was so cold.'

Then he said, in a hard voice, 'You must think I'm stupid.'

'No,' I said. 'It sounds terrifying. Were you and your dad very close?'

He went silent and clenched his hands. 'You think I'm stupid,' he repeated.

'No, I don't.'

'Yes, you fucking do!' he shouted.

He looked up and noticed I was crying. 'Why you crying?' he demanded.

'You – feeling you were buried with your dad.'

He was shocked. 'Sorry,' he said. 'Sorry. Didn't mean to upset you.'

'Did you tell anyone you felt like that?' I said.

'No. Nobody.'

'Have you told anyone since? Your mum?'

His voice hardened again. 'She married again.'

'Soon after?'

He clenched his hands again and mumbled something.

'Sorry,' I said. 'Didn't catch it. Say it slowly.'

'When – she – got – herself – a – new – man,' he said, with immense bitterness.

'Don't you like him?'

He shrugged. 'He's all right. Where's the tea?' he said suddenly. 'I'm a bit hungry.'

We had tea, then prayed. After each visit he would seem deep in thought, and tired, and the walk home, pushing his wheelchair up the hill, was usually completed in silence. Before leaving him with one of the nurses I would ask him if he'd like to come again, and he'd say, 'Yes. When?'

5

It was the start of a pattern of visits. Daniel would come to the house or I would drop in to the home to see him after he got back from work. After a chat, I'd pray with him, usually in silence.

Quite often when I was praying, phrases from scripture would go through my mind: *Your love reaches to heaven and your truth to the skies* was one, from the Psalms. Another snippet was the words of Jesus: *I am with you always, until the end of time.*

I never said any of it aloud but one evening after I'd prayed with him, Daniel put down his cup of tea, looked out of the window and said quietly, 'I am with you always, all the time.'

'What was that you said?' I said, startled.

'Can't remember,' he said. 'Nothing.'

When I took him home early one evening because I had to get ready for the weekly healing group that was held in our house, he asked if he could come to it.

As the matron had made it clear she didn't like 'religious people', I didn't expect to be given permission for Daniel to come, but another member of staff was on duty and said it was fine for Daniel to stay out later, and nice to see him coming home happy.

After the group meeting, Daniel asked me if everyone

there believed in God. I said no, but that I went to a prayer group where everyone did. He said he'd like to go to that as well. Again, permission was given.

In the meantime, he came to the healing group again and proved to be a challenge for some of the others who attended it. A nun was there one week. I didn't know her very well but she seemed a bit subdued, perhaps depressed. Halfway through the evening, Daniel wheeled himself over to her and said, 'Do you believe in God?'

She laughed. 'I'm a nun, Daniel!'

'Do you believe in God?' he repeated.

Her laugh had an uncertain note this time. 'I'm a religious! My whole life is dedicated to the Lord.'

He grabbed her hand and shook it up and down. 'Do – you – *believe* – in – *God*?' he demanded.

She went quiet for a moment, then said, 'Yes.'

Afterwards she said, 'I didn't think I needed to be asked that, but maybe I did.'

One day he asked me, 'When am I going to die?'

'Why would you die any sooner than anyone else?' I asked. 'Are you ill?'

'No. You know. Because of how I am.'

'But that's brain damage, from birth, Daniel. It's not as though you had a disease like...' My mind went blank. I couldn't think of any.

'Muscular dystrophy,' he said helpfully.

I started to laugh. 'You're not that brain damaged either, are you?'

'What do you think of me?' he asked.

'I think you're highly intelligent,' I said, 'and frustrated at not being able to do all the things you want to do.'

'Highly intelligent?' he said. 'Don't make me laugh!'

'Well, I've never had conversations like this with someone who's officially meant to be severely brain damaged,' I said. 'Have you?'

He shrugged. 'Suppose not.'

The other residents in the home where Daniel lived commented that he was becoming quieter, less aggressive. Most of them liked him, but had sometimes been frightened by his violent outbursts. Now he seemed calmer, they said. And happier. From having several fits a week, he had been free of them for six weeks now.

I began to think the Lord might have changed his mind about only giving me failure. But he knew better than me what was ahead.

I had been talking to Daniel about the way he thought and spoke – clearly and incisively – when he was with me or with members of the prayer group, and the contrast when he was with his family or staff at the home. There he still spoke baby talk and pretended to be unable to understand the simplest sentences.

He had also asked us to pray for him to walk, and could now manage about twenty steps at a time. His mother said he hadn't walked since he was seven.

I told him I thought it was time he stopped leading a double life, and let someone know who he was, how deeply he thought about things, how much he understood and what he could do. Would he speak to someone close to him? I knew he was fond of his brother-in-law. Would he talk to him?

He shook his head violently. 'No one,' he said. 'No one must know. Don't tell anybody. Promise.'

I was startled by his vehemence. 'But why not?' I said. 'It's good news. They'll be pleased for you.'

'No, they won't,' he said. 'They want to kill me.'

That sounded like paranoia. 'Of course they don't want to kill you,' I said. 'Your family love you.'

He shook his head. 'They want me to die,' he said.

'Why?' I asked.

'Don't know,' he said. 'Don't understand it myself.'

To change the subject, I picked up the library book that had been chosen for him that week. His family read to him, when they visited. I'd seen Daniel reading himself, and wondered why no one thought it odd that someone considered severely brain damaged read with such obvious focus. Perhaps they thought he didn't understand what he read.

As well as library books – this one was a grisly murder – his family bought him pornographic magazines. They thought it was funny to see him turning the pages and looking at the pictures. To me, it seemed a form of cruelty, hardly likely to make him less frustrated with his life – like dangling a carrot in front of a donkey tethered in a stall, always out of reach.

I asked him if he'd like me to bring him anything else to read. Another book, or comics – whatever he wanted.

'Yes,' he said firmly. 'I want you to bring me a book about the Lord.'

'About God?' I was a bit taken aback.

'Yes. A book about him. Can you get one?'

'Sure. Have you read the gospels?'

He shook his head.

During the week, I called in with a copy of St Luke's Gospel and we started reading it. I read aloud and he followed the line of print with his finger, repeating some of the phrases and words. If he repeated a part more than once, I asked him if he knew what it meant and if he said no, I explained it.

I was beginning to think that brain damage was less of a barrier to understanding the ways of God than a dull spirit – and Daniel's spirit was certainly live and well!

On my next visit, the matron came in and said she wanted to see me in her office. She closed the door and said she had to warn me that she would not tolerate religion. Daniel was being brainwashed, she said. He had his library book and his men's magazines and he was not to be brought religious rubbish to read.

I explained that he'd asked for a book about God.

'Daniel can't ask for anything,' she said. 'He is incapable of making decisions for himself.'

At this point Daniel opened the door and peered round it anxiously.

'What's going on?' he said.

The matron told him to go away. She watched him wheel himself disconsolately down the corridor. Then she told me to go. I could come again, she said, but there was to be no talk about God, no praying, no contact. Daniel would not come to my house any more and I could not go into his room. I could see him in the dining room and read the newspaper with him or play ludo. Was that quite understood?

I said I understood that she was worried. But I wasn't sure what she was worried about.

She said if I couldn't understand that, there was no point in discussing it. If I couldn't accept those rules, I could not see Daniel again.

I began to say that she obviously thought something bad was going on, and perhaps she just needed to know a bit more about me, but she interrupted and said I could either accept her rules or get out.

I said I'd accept whatever terms she was comfortable

with, and asked if I could see Daniel before I went home now, as he seemed anxious. She said no, and not to come back again till next week.

I went home and prayed. And prayed. 'What's going on, Lord? And what do you want me to do?'

Again, a sombre tone. 'Keep going, until you are actually thrown out. Do as they say, and keep praying for Daniel. These are the circumstances he lives in.'

It didn't take long for me to get thrown out.

I called in, on the day arranged with the matron. A nurse showed me into the sitting room and said she would call Daniel in. I waited twenty minutes and asked again. The nurse said she'd go and see.

After being there three-quarters of an hour I went to the office, where the male deputy was sitting in front of the computer. I said I didn't want to rush them, but I had to be home to make my husband's supper in half an hour, and was it convenient for me to see Daniel this evening, or should I come back tomorrow?

He said Daniel wasn't ready, but would be soon. He carried on typing.

I asked if I could put my head round the door of Daniel's room and just let him know I was here and would wait for him in the sitting room? He said OK. He stopped typing and watched me as I walked down the corridor.

Daniel was sitting in his wheelchair, facing the window, which was wide open. It was winter. He was naked, blue with cold, and shivering. He was also embarrassed to be seen with nothing on. I apologized and said I'd fetch a nurse.

I ran back to the male attendant. 'He's got no clothes on and he's freezing,' I told him.

He didn't look up from the keyboard. 'Someone will be with him in a minute.'

'He's blue with cold,' I said.

He shrugged. 'Someone will be along soon.'

I went back to the sitting room and waited. Another twenty minutes.

The man had gone from the office. I walked down the corridor to find a nurse, but there was no one around. I went back to Daniel's room. He was still naked, stone cold, with the window open.

'How long have you been like this?' I asked him.

'Long time,' he said. His teeth were chattering.

I slammed the window closed, opened his wardrobe, found a dressing gown and put it over him, took the duvet off the bed and wrapped it round him, and found his slippers under the bed.

I was kneeling down, pushing his frozen feet into the slippers, when I looked up and saw the attendant in the doorway, smiling unpleasantly.

Two days later I received a note from the matron saying I had failed to respect her rules and would not be allowed to see Daniel any more.

I made two attempts to arrange a meeting with her. She refused both and threatened me with a 'tribunal of officials from social services' if I made contact with Daniel or his family, or any of the staff. I was stunned by this.

My husband advised me to have nothing to do with the home or any 'tribunal'; he said, 'The matron will tell them whatever she wants, in advance, and they'll have already made up their minds; you won't be believed.' And the Lord had only told me to stay as long as I could until forced to go. That point seemed to have been reached. I only hoped Daniel could work out enough of the situation to realize I hadn't abandoned him.

It was several months before I saw Daniel again. One of the other residents, Roger, told me he had been ill. A succession of fits, then kidney trouble, then pneumonia. Several separate admissions to hospital.

'He's home now,' Roger said. 'I expect he'd be glad to see you. Why don't you call in?'

I said I had been told not to, but if he would give Daniel my love and tell him I was thinking of him and praying for him, I'd be grateful.

He asked who had told me not to visit him, and why. I said I didn't understand the reasons, but it wouldn't be right for me to go in without the matron's permission.

'Does Daniel know you're not allowed to see him?' he asked.

I said I thought probably no one had told him. Roger shook his head. 'They're a weird lot,' he said. 'Pity. You did him good. I'll give him your love.'

I saw Daniel one more time. He was in the street, about to be lifted into the van. His head was hanging down and he looked completely defeated. I said hello, and it took a few minutes to register. Then the hand was flung out and he caught my arm and said something.

'Say it again,' I said. 'I didn't catch it.'

He went into the mumbling routine, looking away.

'Quick,' I said. 'You're about to get into the van.'

He looked straight at me and said, 'You left me.'

It was like being stabbed. 'I didn't want to,' I said. 'The matron told me to stay away.'

'What for?' he shouted suddenly.

'I don't know,' I said. 'I didn't understand why.'

'Come along, Danny boy!' said the van driver. 'Up and away with you!'

It must have been shortly afterwards that he was readmitted to hospital, then moved to another one. His friend from the home didn't know where. He was about to move to a new home himself. The matron was taking early retirement, he said, and the home was being closed for refurbishment. Fifteen years later, it still hasn't reopened; it's been standing half-finished and almost deserted for all that time. Maybe the problems there were too deep to be dealt with by refurbishing a building.

I don't know what happened to Daniel. I still don't know now. All I do know is that he has a Father who loves him and knows who he is and what he had to go through. And that the Father alone, of everyone who passed through Daniel's life, would never fail him.

6

The great love affair that is God's chosen form of relationship with us acts as a spotlight on our life. God gives every person a variety of opportunities to let him come into their life and light it up.

Sometimes that seems like a threat. A person may feel he or she has something to hide. They may not understand yet that in God's sphere of thinking, there is no blame. We blame ourselves for what goes on in our life, so we can't see how he is going to come into our life and not cast blame on everything we've done or failed to do.

I began to see that even failed healing is healing.

Even if someone begins to let God have some say in their life, and then slams the door on him – or someone else slams it for them – still, the bit of light that has been allowed in has done something: revealed some truth, some faith or some fear, that was hidden and not accepted.

It's not hard to understand why Daniel's carers might have found him easier to deal with if he was crushed in spirit as well as damaged in body and mind. I could at least see reasons – even if they weren't good ones – why somebody would impede another person's healing. What I found harder to understand was that someone would impede their own.

Why would anyone who had the chance of being well want to stay unwell – even when everyone around them wanted them strong and healthy?

It was Maggie who led me to ponder this one. Again, I don't have the answers – just plenty of questions!

Maggie was a young woman who had backache so bad she had to give up work. Extensive tests on the spine had revealed nothing. The next test proposed was a lumbar puncture. The thought of that made her afraid, and she was looking around for alternatives. She had tried osteopathy, which had not helped, and she was also seeing a naturopath.

Before her friend brought her to meet me, I prayed about what she needed and how to pray for her. I was told not to ask her to show me where the pain was; the source was not in the spine. I was to lay hands on her and pray, and feel where the pain was coming from.

I was not experienced in 'laying on hands' at that stage, but in the few times I had prayed like that, I had sometimes felt pain in the person. Even if I wasn't touching them, just holding my hands over them, there would be some places that felt like a bruise on an apple – vulnerable, too soft.

When Maggie arrived, I was shocked. This was obviously not just a person with a back problem, but a seriously ill young woman. She looked terrible – very thin, pale and shaky, with skin so translucent it had a greenish tinge.

When I laid hands on her, I found no sign of tenderness in or around the spine, only over the joints at either side of it, above the ovaries. When I went straight for this spot, she jumped, and said, 'How did you know that's where the pain is?'

There were more 'soft spots' over the temples and wrists. I asked her if she had ever had epileptic fits, and she said she had in childhood, but didn't have the problem now. But it didn't feel healed, to me. I also asked if she had had sudden stiffness down one side or inability to use her arms or legs. She said no. Her only problem was her back.

I felt she needed a lot of prayer, but there were practical difficulties. She lived some distance away. Praying with her made her relaxed but so weak and sleepy she couldn't stay awake, let alone travel home alone. The journey here and back, plus the effort of shopping, cooking, and looking after herself, would sap all the strength she would receive.

She lived with her sister, so I had a word with her. She was aware that Maggie was ill but had planned a trip abroad and wasn't willing to postpone it for the couple of months that Maggie would need help. Her parents were willing, but over-committed with caring for elderly relatives; they couldn't take on much more, but they would have Maggie home at weekends.

Maggie felt able to drive herself to and from our house, as long as she didn't have to walk. So we evolved a system. She arrived every weekday morning and went straight to bed in our spare room. When she had rested, I would take her something to eat, then pray with her. Then she'd have another rest. Then more prayer, lunch, sleep, then home.

She was anxious to get back to work as soon as possible. She was angry that I kept praying for these 'weak points' in the joints, in the head and in the arms, and wanted me to concentrate on the spine, where the doctor had said the trouble was.

She kept saying, 'There's nothing wrong with me. I'm just a person with a bad back,' but every time I prayed the Lord said there was nothing wrong with the spine itself and that having more tests on it could actually cause paralysis, in her present state. She was very weak and sick.

I told Maggie I could only pray in the way I was given to pray, and asked her to give it the benefit of the doubt for two months – prayer, rest, and no more tests yet. She said one month was the most she would give it. She had booked a holiday abroad then, and if she was well enough by then to go, she would believe this way of healing had something to offer; if not, she would give it up as a bad job.

The Lord told me to agree to her terms, but to add one more period of prayer to the day's schedule. This made for a full day, as other people were coming for healing at the same time. Sometimes there was no break between one person's prayer session and the next one. Still, I reckoned it couldn't do me much harm to be praying all day!

The Lord said Maggie's problem was cancer in the ovaries, which had got into the bone and affected the nearest joints. She was also still prone to fits, and vulnerable to paralysis. I was not to tell her this because it would frighten her; I was just to ask her to be patient for a while, even if I seemed slow. There was nothing that God couldn't heal here but it would take time, because time was what she needed – time and care.

During prayer, Maggie was quiet and receptive. I could feel it making a difference. So could she. But once she got home in the evening, there was a reaction. She would get bouts of aggression, phone up and scream at me: I was a nutter; it was all a waste of time; nothing was helping her.

The next day, she would arrive tense and angry. It could take an hour or two for her to calm down. Then we would pray. Every day I expected she wouldn't come back again, but every day she did. Anger made her resistant; it was harder to pray with her as time went on and I felt a lot of the effort was ineffective, but she continued to accept at least some of it.

The Lord said it was worth persevering unless she shut me out completely. He also told me to tell her not to try to understand his work in terms of the therapies and philosophies she followed: astrology, transcendental meditation, and holistic healing. He told me not to try to talk her out of them, just to warn her they were not the same as the healing he was offering and could cause conflict in her mind – and to tell her that the naturopath she saw was taking drugs and that this impaired his perception.

Maggie refuted all this decisively. There was no conflict, she said, between the healing I believed in and the things she was involved in; it was all the same. And her naturopath would never take drugs; he was always telling her how important it was to put only pure substances into the body.

I suggested she ask him. She came back and reported that he had said he did take drugs, but they 'freed his mind', and didn't impair his perception.

One week she shouted at me for wasting time. Three-quarters of an hour had been spent in silent prayer over her, without any contact. She demanded I laid hands on her spine and cured the 'real problem' immediately. I told her I could either pray in the way God directed me, or not at all. I had no power of my own. He did the healing. He knew what to do. I didn't. She must take it or leave it.

She stayed, but phoned and argued for three hours that evening.

The following week, the Lord told me to change the way of praying now – to use words, to focus on the sore spots on the wrists, and to pray for protection against paralysis.

Maggie was furious. 'Why can't you do it the way you did last week?' she demanded. 'It felt really good! I want you to go on with that!'

'You didn't say that at the time,' I reminded her, but she said, 'Well, I'm saying it now!'

The weather was warm now and Maggie felt well enough to spend her rest times in a deckchair in the garden. Between praying with other people who called to the house, I was doing some gardening one day. I had planted two lupin plants and they were not thriving. Both were infested with whitefly, so heavily the leaves and stems had been stripped bare.

I was about to pull them out, when Maggie said, with a slight sneer, 'Perhaps you should give them some healing! It might work better on plants!'

It was while we were in the next session of prayer that the Lord said, 'Heal one plant. Leave the other one as it is. Let her see.'

I was annoyed. 'I'm not wasting time on a lupin! And how do you heal a plant, anyhow? We've run out of aphid spray!'

'I'll show you. She needs something she can see.'

That evening, I went into the garden. The lupins were a sad sight – naked stalks, whitish and drooping.

'Dig a trench round the one at the front,' the Lord directed. 'Let some air to the roots.'

I knew a bit about gardening, but I'd never heard that one. I dug out a circle around the plant so some of the roots were exposed. I couldn't see that that would do anything. Surely plants need soil?

The next part seemed more logical. 'Lay newspaper around the plant, and brush off the whiteflies on to the paper and throw it away. Then spray the plant with clean water. Do it again tomorrow, and the next day.'

The following week, Maggie was in the garden, reading. I came out with a cup of tea, and she said, 'Is that the same lupin or did you buy another one?'

'It's the same one,' I said.

'What did you do?'

I grinned at her. 'What you told me to. Gave it a bit of healing!'

'How?'

I told her.

'That doesn't count,' she said. 'If you give it all that attention, of course it'll be all right.'

'That's all healing is,' I said. 'The only miracle is love. It's not a magic trick. It takes care, and time.'

She gave me a suspicious look. She'd got the connection.

'Where's the other one?'

I pointed to a brown stem sticking out of the ground. 'Dead.'

'That's not fair!' she said. She looked upset. 'Why does one get all the attention and the other one gets nothing?'

'I don't have unlimited time.'

She sat up. There were tears in her eyes. 'It doesn't

seem right,' she said. 'Some people are worse off than me. Why should I get all this, and they don't?'

'You're here,' I said, 'and they're not. And maybe they couldn't be. It isn't easy, is it – healing? It isn't easy for you.'

'No,' she said. 'People don't realize that,' she said suddenly. 'Especially when I tell them it costs nothing.'

'In a way, it costs you everything,' I told her. 'It did me, when I was being healed. You hand your whole life to God and you have to trust him, or at least give him the benefit of the doubt. It feels like a huge risk. But it isn't.' (For anyone interested in a fuller account of the author's healing see *Don't Ask Me to Believe*.)

It was time, the Lord said, for Maggie to start doing some exercise, loosening and strengthening her back. Maggie refused. It would cripple her, she said. Her spine wasn't strong enough.

She came back the next day and said something strange had happened the previous evening. She had been lying on her bed at home and had made up her mind that she wasn't going to do any exercises; she wasn't fit. A few minutes later, her back started arching and straightening. She said it was like waves of power going through her. It wasn't a strain on her back, and it felt very good – very healthy. Her back was exercising itself.

The Lord was about to send Maggie another sign of how he operated. Maggie still believed that healing was psychological or depended on spiritual enlightenment – on studying and understanding and being 'tuned in'. She said she supposed it couldn't work for babies, or mentally handicapped people, because you couldn't explain things to them. I said they were easier to heal;

they left it to their spirit to understand things, instead of relying on their intellect. They had not lost their sense of God yet.

One morning when Maggie was there, a friend called round and asked if she could leave the baby with me and if I could 'do my stuff on her'. The older child had swung on the cradle this morning and catapulted the baby out on to the floor. She had fallen on her head and hadn't stopped crying since. My friend would call back after taking the older child to nursery and, if I couldn't do anything, would take the baby to the doctor.

The baby was crying hard. I realized I hadn't asked the mother where the child had hit her head, so I felt for the 'bruised apple' feeling and found it on the left temple. As soon as I held my hand over it, the baby turned her head to one side and fell asleep instantly. I kept praying till I felt the soft spot firm up and, as I said under my breath, 'That's it now,' the baby woke up and smiled.

'OK,' Maggie said, 'I'm convinced. It's not psychological. Or else babies have a far deeper psyche than I'd realized!'

The month was nearly up. Maggie was looking much better; she had put on weight, had more colour, and was moving and bending more easily. But she swore she was no better and I had wasted her time.

Her parents phoned and said they were delighted with her progress – but were afraid to say anything because she bit their heads off. Her friends were relieved to see her looking better, and one of them offered her a part-time job. She could come in when she liked, do however much work she could cope with, and rest in an adjoining room when she needed to. She refused angrily.

She was a sick person, she said, unable to work.

The day arrived for the holiday she had booked, and she went away. At the end of the fortnight she returned, brown, plump and glowing – a picture of health. While she was telling me about her holiday – she had been swimming and dancing – she was doing the washing-up, bending and stretching and putting dishes away. I said it was lovely to see her so happy and well. She immediately stopped, sank into a chair, scowling, and said I needn't think she was better or that I had done anything. She was just the same as she had been – a person with a back problem.

The aggression got so bad that the Lord said he would not allow me to go on praying with her unless she tried to deal with it. Healing was not to be at another person's expense. I could make allowances, while she was ill and confused and frightened and couldn't help it, but now it was time for her to make a choice.

Healing is constructive; it builds up the person's spiritual resources so the body can get on with its natural work of repairing itself. For Maggie to go on being so destructive would not only pull her away from God – the only source of real health – but it would have a bad effect on my health. At this stage, I was still recovering from my own illness, and would produce lumps and growths and sometimes faint, under too much stress. Her anger was beginning to wear me down.

I told Maggie this. She complained I didn't care about her, that I was starting to give her less time and to give priority to other people's appointments for prayer instead of dropping everything when she felt unwell. I said she was no longer the weakest or neediest of the people who came. She denied it furiously.

One day, she was driving from home to our house, when her car stopped at a roundabout. There was nothing wrong with the car; she just found she couldn't drive on. She went home and phoned me, puzzled. 'I just can't get there,' she said. 'Something's stopping me.'

I suggested she phoned me again in a couple of days, and we'd take it from there, make another appointment if she wanted.

That was the last time I heard from her.

Friends occasionally brought news. She had gone into hospital and had more tests on her back including a lumbar puncture which had paralysed her for a week. She had recovered from the paralysis; the doctors had found nothing wrong with her spine, and further tests revealed nothing anywhere else.

She had gone back to her full-time job. Her father had died. She was in a relationship and had had a baby. She was still saying healing was rubbish and I was some fruitcake who believed that God healed people. But she was undeniably healthy.

'So it wasn't a failure, this time, then?' I asked God.

'It is a failure until she forgives,' was the answer. 'She forgave the doctors for the paralysis after the lumbar puncture. But she won't forgive herself, until she forgives you. Until then, however healthy she is physically, her spirit can't be healed.'

It was a failure, then, though it looked – and must have felt – like success.

And the ones that felt like real failures – like Daniel – had some elements of success.

Physically, Daniel was not healed. Nor was Alicia, or Michelle. But then the Lord had said right from the start that they were strong souls, not to be seen as victims of sickness and disability. He described them as 'exhausted missionaries' – healing many people very successfully, but without enough support. They had become overloaded.

My role, he said, was not to take their suffering away from them. It was their work. I couldn't do it instead of them, or stop them from doing it. I was only being asked to share the load, including the rejection and humiliation imposed on them.

Every person who shared the life of Daniel or Alicia or Michelle had a choice: they could either make life easier for them, or harder. They could only make it easier by consulting God and asking how to help. If they tried to decide alone, they could intend to make life easier for them but in fact make it harder. They could believe they were giving, but end up taking from them.

The choices they made for Daniel, or whichever 'sick person's' life they shared, would be the same choices they were making for themselves. If they were choosing not to accept God's first offer, but to make some other choice for themselves, which in the long run would make their life harder, then they could only do that for others as well.

You can't treat somebody better than you treat yourself.

I noticed that when people were very aggressive towards others, it was only a fraction of the fury they felt towards themselves. They were intensely self-destructive.

It is hard to stand back and watch someone destroy themselves.

I saw a friend die of cancer. She had left our prayer group because one of the members kept praying about a subject that made her uncomfortable. She expressed extreme hatred for this person, and refused to come back to the meetings.

The Lord told me to talk to her about addiction. At this stage, she had not been diagnosed as having cancer, but she wasn't looking good. He said she had two major addictions that she was hiding from everyone. He told me to ask her about them. She admitted to one, and said she knew she had to do something about it. I offered to pray with her, and she accepted.

She called me again a long time later, when she became ill. I asked her about the addiction, but she said it was no longer a problem. With her consent, I prayed with her about both addictions. She denied the second, and repeated that the first had now been dealt with.

Her sickness continued. The Lord told me the cancer was not the root problem, only a symptom of a deeper self-destruction. My role was to continue to pray about the first addiction. He said it was not cured, and her way of avoiding the second had not been his way; it was destructive to her health and had contributed to her present sickness.

By the time she died, he said she had no unfinished business in this life. It had been dealt with. She was free of addiction and had let go of the hatred she had focused on certain people. But it had been at great cost.

It was only many months after her death that I heard that her addiction had continued, almost to the very end of her life, when she had no choice.

I couldn't see any good news at all in her story. It seemed a life of evasion, and slavery to other masters. The Lord said otherwise.

'She made her own choices, using her gift of free choice. She stopped blaming people for her own decisions. She stopped hating them for their weaknesses, which reflected her own, so she stopped hating herself.

She was separated from her destructive addictions when she died.'

'But death is the ultimate destruction!' I argued.

'No,' was the answer. 'Who told you that one? Death is powerless. She invited me into her life, and although she kept pushing me away, enough of my love affected her. She's free now to enjoy the rest of her life. Eternally. What's the problem?'

I don't know what the problem is, except that her choices didn't suit me. Or her children, or her friends. But then, they didn't have to. It was her life.

And if God didn't blame her, and she is happy now, how could anyone complain?

7

None of this reasoning is going to stop me – or anyone – grieving over the loss of someone who died at a time when their life on earth seemed to have so much more to offer. Nor is it going to stop anyone feeling distressed when someone, in spite of heartfelt prayer, continues to be ill, disabled or injured, when they really don't want to be.

But grieving is not loss of faith in God. He never told me not to grieve over anyone. On one occasion he said, when someone was dying and everyone was trying hard to be positive – at least when they were with him – 'Grieve, you must grieve for him. But don't worry about him. I will look after him.'

If, as God says, everyone knows him deep down because everyone has come from him and is on their way back to him, that doesn't mean we understand what is happening to us, or to others, in this life. It may be only after death that any of us will finally let go of the world's way of seeing every suffering as tragedy and every pleasure as worth having, and start to see life God's way.

All the episodes in this book can be explained away. So can all the episodes in the Jewish and Christian Bible. Psychology, philosophy, other theologies, medical theory, parapsychology – all can offer their own way of analysing these incidents to fit into their own realm of knowledge.

But in the end, is it useful to try and explain? Trying to fit God into categories of human understanding is like trying to pour a rainbow into an egg-cup.

We're going to have to wait, like it or not, till the moment God shows us our small fragment of life in the light of his whole creation, in the scale of eternity. Till then, we're like children trying to do a jigsaw puzzle when we don't have all the pieces and have lost the lid of the box with the picture on it.

There are moments, though – always unexpected – when a sudden, breathtaking glimpse of the reality of God breaks into our everyday lives. One happened to me a week ago.

In my morning prayer, I'd been reading the account of Jesus talking to his followers for the last time before he was crucified, at the Last Supper. He'd said, 'I've been longing to share this meal with you, because it's the last time we're going to eat together until we all meet up again in the kingdom of heaven.'

It got me thinking: if I knew it was going to be the last time I was going to do anything, even eat dinner, then that event would take on enormous significance. And if, in fact, our life here is going to pass into eternity, then everything we do does actually have that kind of significance. After all, today is the one and only – and last – chance I have of living today's events.

From there, I'd started wondering what I would do today if it was going to be my last day on earth. Clear up any unfinished business, probably; stop putting off things I'd meant to do for ages and get on and do them. There was quite a long list of possibilities!

What I chose to do, as it was a beautiful sunny

autumn morning, was to go to the garden centre, buy some winter-flowering plants, and go and plant them on a friend's grave.

The cemetery is a nice peaceful place, full of squirrels and magpies and jays. Living in London, there aren't many places where you can find a bit of space and peace and quiet. My friend's grave is near the back, by the railway line. Because it's isolated, I'd been advised not to go in there alone, but it's permitted to drive the car in there and park it near the grave, so I felt quite safe. Besides, I have a good guardian angel who quite enjoys the occasional challenge!

I was pottering around with a trowel and a fork, supposedly praying, but distracted with thoughts like, 'Where did all these weeds come from?' and, 'I wonder if that plant has had it or if it's worth leaving in?' when a man walked by. I said good morning. People often walk round the graveyards; there aren't many parks.

A minute later he walked back, slowly, looking at me.

I reminded myself I was meant to be praying, and stopped thinking about weeds. It seemed a bit strange that the man had turned back.

My imagination kicked in. I'd written a novel, *Eldred Jones, Lulubelle and the Most High*, in which a woman got raped in a graveyard just like this one. I'd based the description on this very spot in this very cemetery. And hadn't I been thinking this morning about how I would spend my last day on earth? Was that prophetic?

I wondered if secateurs would be any good for stabbing anyone who got nasty. I dropped them back in the bag quickly. I didn't want to stab anybody – or be stabbed.

Those were my own thoughts. If you start expecting

trouble where there is none, it's like inviting it. I felt I'd do better to concentrate on God's thoughts.

People tending other graves had often come over to chat, on other occasions when I was in the cemetery, and the Lord had told me to be friendly but not to let anyone stop me from what I was there for; it was a place to pray. I got on with saying my prayers. And got on with the planting. The man had walked on by now.

When I took the watering can and walked over to the tap, I saw him sitting on a tombstone not far away, watching.

As I was digging the hole for the first plant, he came over and stood a few yards away. There was suddenly a tension in the atmosphere. I felt uneasy. Maybe the man was troubled in his mind – had come into the cemetery hoping for peace and hadn't found it. Was he hoping to settle instead for dumping his turmoil on someone who seemed at peace?

I wished I was wearing jeans. In a short skirt, it was awkward to go round to the other side of the grave and crouch down to put the plants in. I stayed standing, on the far side of the grave, and leaned across. I tried to work slowly, calmly. Maybe all he needed was calming down.

He came over and stood the other side of the grave. His attitude was intimidating. This didn't seem like a man who wanted peace. I didn't look up and carried on working, and praying. 'Lord,' I said silently, 'do I just carry on as I am? Or run for the car, or what? Tell me, please. Now!'

The man was not calming down. Impatience and anger were coming from him. I found my hands shaking as I patted another plant into place.

It struck me that the danger lay in the fact that he saw me as a woman alone in an isolated place. I knew God was there; he didn't. And I knew that the friend who had died, whose grave it was, had not buzzed off to some far-off outer-space heaven but just moved into a deeper dimension of living, closer to God – and closer to all the people he had been close to on earth. So he was also here. I was not alone. But this man was going to treat me as though I was.

'Lord, I need to know what to do now,' I prayed again. But fear can block the ears. I couldn't hear an answer, just a sense that there was no cause for fear. Any fear is groundless. If today was my time to die, I would die. If suffering was necessary, I would suffer. If not, it wouldn't happen. But my hands were still shaking.

The man said something in a rough tone of voice. I didn't understand his accent.

'Sorry?' I said.

He repeated it angrily, pointing at the grave. 'What's that flower?'

This wasn't about flowers. He wasn't here for the gardening, and I had a strong feeling that whereas you can sometimes calm a person down by talking to them, on this occasion any kind of conversation would be taken advantage of.

I decided to ask my friend to help me hear the Lord. It was his grave, after all, and I doubted he'd be too pleased if my brains were bashed out over all his nice new plants!

'Give me a hand here, would you?' I said silently, and immediately it came into my mind, 'Make it more obvious to him what you're here for.'

So, instead of answering the man's question, I

dropped the trowel into the bag, went up to the headstone of the grave and put my hand on it, then made the sign of the cross over myself, turned away from the man and started to pray – in silence, but I felt it was obvious enough what I was doing.

I felt something like shock hit him. The waves of agitation and anger that had been coming from him stopped, and he froze to the spot.

Then something else changed. It was a lovely sunny day, but the light suddenly became much clearer and whiter. Every gravestone was rimmed in light. Then the air changed. It was as though heaven came down on earth. It's hard to explain, and I know it sounds strange and over-imaginative. But peace is not something the mind can imagine when it's in a state of fear. It can only imagine the worst. This was better than anything I could imagine!

The air was thick with peace. It hung over everything, and felt like a blanket wrapped around me. I felt totally cared for – and as though the man was also being taken care of. The peace he could not get from being in the cemetery, and could not get by taking mine from me, the Father was giving him, free.

The thought crossed my mind that perhaps he was a Muslim. Turning to face another direction and making the sign of the cross may have been gestures he could recognize as symbols of prayer, though they were not the same symbols used by Muslims. But I was sure that he recognized God in this and that he could also feel something going on. He still hadn't moved.

I prayed simply, using standard prayers – the Our Father who art in heaven, the Hail Mary, and the Glory be to the Father. Then I made the sign of the cross again.

The man was standing between me and the car. There was no other way out except past him.

I picked up the bag with the gardening tools and the tray with the rest of the plants and, without looking at him, walked past him. He didn't move.

I opened the car door, put the things in, got in, closed the door and started the engine. The man was still rooted to the spot. He didn't turn round or move.

Only when I was driving out of the cemetery did I look back and see him walking slowly away in the other direction. He looked peaceful.

On the way home, I had the car radio on. A man was talking about fear. We all have fear, he said, but we have to overrule it; if you don't, it will rule your whole life.

It reminded me of something in one of the letters of St Paul, in the New Testament. He said, 'Where there is fear, love has not yet been made perfect. Perfect love casts out fear.'

It's not possible, in human terms, to feel love for someone while they are deliberately intimidating you or when you face the threat of assault, out of reach of human help. The most I could manage, on that occasion, was to remain sure that God loved me, that he loved my friend who died and who still prays for me, and that he loved the man who was in such turmoil that for a while he didn't care if he stole another person's peace of mind.

It's only God whose love is perfect enough to deal with fear. When I got home, I thanked him.

I thanked my friend as well. But I told him to make the most of the flowers on his grave, because there was *no way* I was going in there again to bring him any more!

8

A friend of mine was in hospital, with a blood clot in her leg. She could feel it travelling up past her abdomen, and when it reached her lung her breath stopped and she could feel herself losing consciousness. She was aware of a nurse shaking her and a doctor running and tipping the bed at an angle and hitting her. She felt as though she was being beaten up.

Later in the day, she was sitting up in bed and the doctor came to see her.

'I'm glad to see you're OK,' he said. 'You had me worried!'

'Do you mind if I ask you a question?' she said.

'Go ahead.'

'Are you afraid of dying?'

He pulled a face. 'Yes,' he said. 'Like everyone else.'

'I'm not,' she said. 'I trust God and I know I'm not going to go before my time. I could feel your panic when you were resuscitating me. If that happens again, don't give me your fear of death, or you'll frighten the life out of me!'

Death, in God's terms, seems to be a non-event. If someone is making strides towards him in this life, death is probably one further stride in their progress. But there's no point having faith in death as a major spiritual event. In itself it's only a stage in anyone's life. If a person is making no moves towards God in this life, they're unlikely to find that death carries them a giant leap forward in spiritual enlightenment.

There has been only one time when God has asked me to pray with somebody who had died. 'Call her,' he said, 'and invite her to come back to life.'

There's no need at this point to fast-forward through the pages to find out the outcome. I was still in the time of my 'ministry of failure'! But there was some sign of life, and a sign for me at least that even after the moment of death, God hasn't changed his system – he still gives us, and still respects our, free choice.

The girl was fourteen. She came from a close family of practising Christians, and lived in a parish a few miles away. The family's priest, a Father Matthew, was a former seminary colleague of Father Nathan, one of the priests in the area where I live. This Father Matthew phoned him late one night, in some distress. He knew the family quite well, and had just held the funeral of an aunt who had died. She had been ill for some years and had been expected to die. Then, a few days afterwards, the eldest daughter of the family, who was also ill, but not considered terminal, died suddenly.

He was trying to console the family and prepare for the eldest daughter's funeral, when the fourteen-year-old daughter, Mina, also died. She was apparently in perfect health, had never had any illness in her life, and the family was numb with grief and shock. Father Matthew himself was crying and asked for Nathan's support.

Nathan asked me and another friend, Ben, to pray, and to share with him any guidance we received. Both of us prayed, and felt the same prompting – to go and pray with the girl and treat it as shock, not as the end of the story. And let Father Matthew pray from a distance, not with the girl and with us. His own shock would communicate itself. The best thing would be for Father Nathan to stay with Father Matthew and pray with him.

I had one other instruction – during the night, keep the girl's body warm. Cover her up with a blanket. We would go there in the morning and pray with her, with the family if they would agree to come with us.

Nathan got back to us. The girl's body was now in the undertakers' chapel. He had balked at asking the family to put a cover over her. They would think it strange, he said. Nor could he guarantee to keep Father Matthew away from her. Matthew was not comfortable with the idea of strangers coming to pray with 'his' people. If we wanted to pray with her, he would have to be there.

The parents had not agreed to share in the prayer. But Mina's brother, who was seventeen, wanted to be there. He said he would meet us in the morning at the undertakers'.

Nathan told us that Mina and her brother had always been close. When their elder sister died, and then Mina, he had felt himself starting to go too, he said. He had the feeling of death sucking them all in, one after the other. But he had managed to resist.

We went back to the Lord and prayed again.

Agree to their arrangements, he said. The brother has faith. Nathan will stand between you and the priest; so if Matthew won't stay out of the room, just leave him to Nathan. Don't take on his way of thinking.

The three of us – Father Nathan, Ben and I – drove to the funeral parlour the next morning. We were shown into a waiting room and started to pray in silence while we waited for the others to arrive. Mina's brother came in, very pale, but he greeted us warmly and thanked us for coming. He said last night was the first night he had been able to sleep since his sisters had died.

He was eager to go in and start praying with Mina, but Nathan said we must wait for Father Matthew to arrive.

When Matthew arrived, he shook hands with Nathan but seemed cold towards Ben and me. Nathan told us afterwards he had said he didn't see why we had to be there – ordinary laypeople. It was the priests' job to deal with death, and to pray with people.

We had to wait a while before the undertaker called us into the chapel of rest. Father Matthew perched on the arm of the chair where Mina's brother was sitting, leaning over him and talking in a low voice into his ear. He looked as though he was leaning on him for support. The boy looked drained and anxious now. Father Matthew was telling him the arrangements for Mina's burial.

We were called into the chapel, and the undertaker took the lid off the coffin.

For her funeral, Mina had been dressed as a child – in her white First Communion dress, which must have fitted her when she was seven. She was fourteen now.

Ben and I stood by the coffin, with Nathan behind us. Mina's brother came to join us, but Father Matthew held him back and stood with him by the wall, whispering to him.

We prayed silently.

'Jesus,' I prayed, 'this is your child. Why has she died? Is it just shock at her sister's death? Does she want to wake up now? And would the family cope if she did? Or would they disown her – treat her as someone who brought some strange event into their life?'

He told me to look at the brother. I turned and saw that although Father Matthew was still holding his arm and trying to get his attention, his whole attention was focused on his sister's face. He was praying for her, it seemed, with every fibre of his body. If his sister came back to life, and people treated her as an oddity, she would need someone to stand up for her. And he would be the one. I felt sure of it.

I turned back to the girl and the Lord said, 'Talk to her.'

So I said to her, silently, 'Hi, Mina. I'm Clare. We've come to pray with you. You look very cold to me. Would you like to wake up and get warm?'

Nothing.

'Lord, why am I talking to a dead person?' I asked. 'She can't hear me, can she?'

'Keep going.'

I noticed that her hands, which were clasped together around a child's white rosary, were blue. The fingers, under the fingernails, were colourless. Bloodless. The blood had stopped flowing around her body.

I went to stretch out my hand. Jesus had said that in him, if we believe, we are all one body. I would connect the tips of my fingers to hers and ask for his blood to flow through us both – for my living blood supply to somehow connect with hers and get the flow going.

The words of the Eucharist went through my mind: 'This is my blood. Take it.'

'This is my blood,' I said to the girl. 'Here, take it. Help yourself.'

Her voice was high and clear. And shocked. 'Is that what it means?'

'Oh, yes,' I said, still silently. 'It's real. Jesus gives his blood to us. And we can share what he gives us. So go for it. Help yourself.'

As I reached my hand out towards hers though, the voice said sharply, 'Don't you dare!'

'Lord, what's going on?' I prayed.

'Keep talking to her,' he said. 'She has a choice.'

At this point Father Matthew, who was shuffling about restlessly, came over and said something to Father Nathan, who had his hand on my shoulder, praying for me.

Nathan leaned forward. 'He wants us to start saying prayers,' he whispered. 'He doesn't like this silence.'

'I'm praying!' I whispered back.

'I know!' he said. 'But do it his way!'

He started praying the rosary, aloud. Ben, who had also been praying intently in silence, joined him and Matthew. I thought that was enough voices to be going on with.

'Why don't you want to wake up?' I said to the girl.

The words came so rapidly they were more like a single thought. I had a picture of Mina's family. They were immigrants, she was telling me, still feeling like visitors to this country, unsure of being accepted. The priests were an important source of support. Grief and tragedy they could accept. At present the family were an object of sympathy. But rising from death, the priest would see as very weird. Her parents would be treated as pariahs – the one thing they feared and had tried to avoid since coming to live here.

'It would be a nine days' wonder,' I tried to reassure her. 'People would soon find some way of explaining it away. They'd say a mistake was made; you hadn't really died after all; that kind of thing. People know how to hold on to their comfortable ideas. And what about you? You have a life ahead of you, at your age. Don't you want to do something exciting with it?'

She showed me another picture. An atmosphere of sadness in the house. Photos of her dead sister and her aunty, like a shrine. And an image of herself walking down the street. Pushing a pram.

She had no ambitions really, she said. Life at home seemed fearful and the world outside cold. She could see herself shaming the family, falling for somebody for the sake of a little comfort, having a baby. That was the only thing she could think of that she would like. But that would bring shame on her parents.

'Look at your brother,' I said. 'He'd have you back. He'd love you, whatever you did. Why don't you open your eyes, and let him give you a big hug?'

My hand was halfway towards her eyes. I could feel heat pouring out towards her face.

'No!' she said sharply. 'No!'

Nathan caught hold of my shoulder and pulled me back.

'Go outside now,' he said. 'I'll catch up with you.'

He went and stood by the girl's head and blessed her.

I turned to go. I felt sad and confused. What was the point in being here, coming all this way, if it wasn't what the girl wanted herself?

All I heard was, 'You gave her a choice. She didn't know she had the right to decide.'

'Are you sure?' I said to the girl, as I left the chapel. 'You don't want to change your mind?'

No response.

'OK,' I said. 'I'll see you later, when it's my time to

go. It's been nice meeting you, and I'll look forward to seeing you again.'

A sudden view of her face, though she was out of my range of sight now, in the coffin. A pretty face, smiling. Alive.

'See you later. Thank you!'

Ben wasn't happy when we got out into the street.

'Matthew was praying that nothing would happen,' he told Nathan.

'I know,' Nathan said. 'He has his own burdens to carry.'

'The girl's brother believed,' said Ben. 'Why did you decide to leave? I really thought she was going to wake up, at one point.'

'I thought Clare was going to go,' said Nathan. 'She went stone cold. I don't want another funeral.'

Ben smiled. 'She's died before now and come back to life. It's become a bit of a habit!'

Nathan nodded. 'I know. But I don't think it was a waste. I felt, when I blessed her, that the girl was at peace. I think we did all we were meant to do. I feel it's all right now.'

It was very quiet, on the way home. We all seemed to have a lot to think about.

9
CHAPTER

Ben had doubts about letting people decide they didn't want to be healed.

The prayer group had begun holding monthly healing services; the members, in twos, prayed with anyone who wanted us to. One of those who came over to Ben and me was Steven, an eight-year-old boy with cerebral palsy. He was in a wheelchair and wanted to walk.

We began praying with him and he walked a little, but his attention was constantly distracted; he swung round to look at everyone and couldn't keep his balance, so we sat down to pray some more. Ben felt the Holy Spirit telling him to pray for me and leave me to pray with the child. So he put his hand on my shoulder and prayed, and I put my hands on Steven's legs and prayed for him.

I had my eyes closed, but Ben noticed Steven's expression change and asked him what was happening.

'I can feel moving,' he said. 'In my legs.' His face was screwed up as though he was trying not to cry.

'On the outside of your legs or inside?' Ben asked him.

'Inside,' he said. 'Something moving.'

'Has that ever happened before?'

'No.'

'Well, that's a good sign! Your legs are coming back to life!'

'I don't like it,' he said.

'I think we should keep going,' Ben said. 'How about it, Steven? Shall we have one more try?'

Steven shook his head. 'Can I go home?' he asked me.

'Yes.'

'Why don't you take a break, Steven?' Ben suggested. 'Go back and sit with your aunt for a while, and think about it?'

He said he wanted to go to the toilet, so we called his aunt over and she took him out. By the time they came back, we were praying with somebody else, but we asked her if she'd mind waiting a moment.

'What did you decide?' Ben asked Steven.

'I want to go home.' He still looked as though he was going to cry.

I gave him a hug and said, 'We're here every month. Come any time you want.'

He came back the following month. 'I want to walk now.'

We did the same as before, but with no reaction. Steven kept thumping his legs and saying, 'Nothing! No movement, nothing!' The tears this time were tears of frustration.

Ben said afterwards, 'We should have kept going, the first time. He might have been scared to start with, but he would have got over it. And he would have got what he wanted.'

The Lord offered alternatives. Steven's faith wasn't quite as strong as might have been expected from an eight-year-old. I was given prayers for him and for his brother to say. There were also exercises for Steven to do with his parents, because some of his problem with walking, the Lord said, was to do with mental focus. His attention was easily distracted. The exercise, to do every day, was to walk step by step, facing his mother or father or brother, holding their hands and keeping his eyes on their face. If his eyes wandered away from theirs, they were to tell him.

After a few months, a friend of the family told me they were not doing the prayers or the exercises with the child; the parents were tired and couldn't find the time. I offered to do it instead, if they could bring Steven over to the house sometimes, but they never got round to it. He kept asking them, but it just wasn't within their faith. They couldn't believe it would be worth the effort.

I found it hard to understand that if someone, at the point of starting to be healed, lost their nerve and wanted it to stop, they wouldn't be offered that opportunity again – or not in the same way.

I felt that if I was God I wouldn't have done it that way! I would tell the person that if they said no today, they could come back the following week.

But perhaps that would have put pressure on them. Maybe it is more than a momentary fear that makes someone refuse the very opportunity they have been hoping and praying for, and the reason for the refusal comes from deep in their spirit. And maybe it is a good reason. If they are healing other people, perhaps those people would not accept anything more from them if they made such an unexpected leap from sickness to health. I don't know.

There were a couple of other occasions when people

drew back from the edge of receiving the healing they said they wanted.

Ellen was an elderly blind lady who used to visit one of our neighbours one day a week. They were both practising Christians, and the neighbour asked me if I'd go in and pray with them both every week. We had some good prayer times, very peaceful. But I kept getting the feeling that Ellen might be healed.

I asked her if she had been blind from birth, and she said no, from the age of five. The doctor had told her that she would never see again. I asked her if she would be willing to pray to get back her sight, and she said she would.

So I asked a lady from our prayer group, called Carrie, to come and pray with me and to pray about whether I was asking for the right thing. She was an elderly West Indian lady, a long-distance marathon pray-er of great kindness and perseverance. She came and met the two women, and afterwards said, 'I am sure that lady can see. We should pray for her sight.'

So we went for it. Carrie laid hands on Ellen's head, and I held mine over one of her eyes. Both Ellen's eyes were cloudy and there was no dividing rim between the pupil and the iris – just an indefinite circle of darkness in the centre of the white eye.

I started with the eye that didn't look as bad as the other. You could just about see where the pupil was. The other eye didn't seem to have one at all.

As I prayed over the eye, I saw a change. The pupil was clearly distinguished from the iris, and appeared shiny: there was a light in it. The eye looked at me. It looked focused. I was looking Ellen straight in the eye.

'Ellen, how do you feel?' I asked.

'Fine,' she said. 'Very much at peace.'

'But... oh, right. I'm going to pray for the other eye now, OK?'

'Yes, fine.'

I held my hand over the 'bad eye'. The first eye continued looking at me. I began to feel a bit strange.

The second eye cleared as the first one had. A clear black pupil emerged from the indistinct mess, and separated itself from the iris, which took on a light colour. There was light shining out of the whole eye – out of both eyes.

Ellen was looking straight at me with both eyes – looking at me looking back at her. Her eyes were completely focused. I moved my head to one side. The eyes followed me. I moved the other way. Her eyes moved again.

'Ellen,' I said, 'do you believe God can heal anyone of anything?'

'Oh yes,' she said. 'I do believe.'

Her eyes, looking at me, were bright and intelligent.

'Do you believe God can heal you of blindness and let you see?' I said.

'The doctor told me I'd never see again,' she said decisively.

With horror, I watched both eyes cloud over again and the pupil disappear into the iris, which took on a muddy colour and an irregular outline.

When we got outside, Carrie said to me, 'Clare, that woman could see.'

'I know,' I said. 'She was looking straight at me. What do we do now?'

'Nothing,' said Carrie. 'Nothing you can do, if she won't believe.'

'Nothing I do works out!' I said in despair. 'Every time someone gets healed, it gets thrown away!'

She smiled and quoted at me, '"Unless a grain of wheat falls to the ground and dies, it remains a single grain and can't bear fruit." You are going to bear a lot of fruit for the Lord, believe me.' She gave me a bear hug and went to get her bus home.

Amy was in her late twenties and had already had an operation to bypass the bowel, and had an ileostomy; that is, a hole had been made in her side, at the level of the higher part of the stomach, and all the refuse that would normally travel through the intestine and out of the bowel came out here, into a bag which she had to change every day.

It was a lot to cope with, as well as bringing up children and dealing with the worry that the disease might progress. Her one ambition was to get well enough for the operation to be reversed and for her to regain normal use of the bowel. The doctors had said there was a chance, but no guarantee.

She was thin and nervous, looked very tired, talked very fast, and never sat still for a minute. If she was going to get well, she would need rest and peace. But with two children, that didn't seem possible.

Then her sister volunteered to come and stay with her. Amy could take to her bed, and her sister would bring her all her meals, do the housework, and look after the children. This was terrific!

So Amy learned to rest, and I went round and prayed with her twice a week, and ministers from the church brought her the Eucharist and prayed with her every day.

I had asked the Lord how to pray for her, and was

given a simple formula: 'Pray for the soul to be healed, and for the hole to be sealed!'

Amy was happy with this.

After a while, she showed me a change. When she changed the bag every day, she had to put a seal against the skin and attach the bag to that. To make sure it exactly fitted the stoma (the hole in her side) she had to cut a hole the same size in the centre of the seal. For several days now, she told me, she had had to cut the hole a bit smaller every day. The difference now was quite noticeable. The hole was sealing itself up.

I was delighted, but Amy seemed worried.

'Where's the stuff going to come out, if the hole closes up?'

It was God who was doing the healing, I reminded her. He knew about that. He wouldn't half-heal her, leaving her with a worse problem than before. His healing was total – and safe.

A few days later, the hole was still closing up – and she had been to the toilet normally.

'Wonderful!' I applauded.

Amy was more worried still. 'The doctors told me I can't use the back passage at all.'

'Did it hurt?' I asked.

'No. But I'm not meant to go to the toilet. Not since the operation.'

'You've been praying for the operation to be reversed,' I reminded her, 'so that you can go back to normal.'

'But the doctors have to do it! It'll take another operation.'

'Maybe God is doing it for you,' I suggested.

'I can't cope with this,' she said. 'I want it to be done in the normal way.'

'Normal for us, or normal for God?'

'Normal for me. Normal.'

'You can pray for the healing to stop if you want. You're always the one in control,' I told her. 'God would never do anything you wouldn't want.'

'Yes, but he wouldn't be pleased if I said no, would he?'

'He wouldn't be pleased if you're scared sick of what's happening,' I pointed out. 'That wouldn't be healing, would it?'

So she asked me to pray for the healing to cease, and the next day the hole stayed the same size and didn't shrink any more.

The doctors said the operation couldn't be reversed and that she would require a further operation, to remove the rectum. She would never again go to the toilet normally.

Then the stoma kept leaking and the specialist said it was too flat and should be refashioned, and possibly moved to the other side. She was given a raised stoma. In time, it grew and took on the appearance of a third breast, because some of the flesh they had used to create the new stoma was breast tissue. Amy, not unnaturally, found this distressing.

She began to experience discomfort and pain, but the doctor thought this was not connected and that she needed a hysterectomy. So the womb was removed, but it was found to be quite healthy and the operation turned out to have been unnecessary, and the pain continued.

Amy coped with all this suffering. She prayed, and her faith grew. She went to healing services and joined our prayer group, and although the physical problem was never reversed, she grew stronger and more peaceful.

She started going to the gym and built up her physical strength.

She was also a tower of strength to other people: she helped a single mother care for her twin children, and nursed two people with cancer through their last months of life. She took on a part-time job, and her confidence grew. She is always beautifully dressed, outgoing, and cheerful. She looks the picture of health and confidence.

Earlier this year, she had the opportunity to go on holiday and had no one to go with, so she asked me if I'd like to go. It was a lovely week, in a lovely place, sunny and relaxing. Easy. And Amy was easy to be with.

Towards the end of the holiday, we were sitting out on the balcony one evening and she said, 'You know, it occurred to me that this is the first time in years that I've been on my own with you for any length of time. I wondered if this would be the time for my healing.'

'Healing from what?' I said. 'You're one of the strongest people I know!'

'The stoma. I cope with it, but it's a hassle – changing the bag and everything. I'd really like to get rid of it, once and for all.'

I asked her if she remembered the first time – fifteen years ago – when the stoma had shrunk. She did.

'I've never liked to ask you,' I said, 'but why did you say no? Was it fear, because it felt so unnatural? Or did you believe it wouldn't turn out right and you'd be left in a worse state, unless the doctors did the operation?'

'I don't know,' she said slowly. 'I've thought about it. It did feel frightening, but it wasn't that. I was afraid of what people would say.'

'What they would say about what?'

'About me. That if I got healed, they'd see me as some kind of freak. Call me a religious maniac or something.'

'Like me?' I suggested, and we both laughed.

'You were used to it,' she said.

'Well, I am now!'

I told her what I'd thought about Steven – how I couldn't see why he couldn't be healed at the following month's healing service when he'd said no at the first one. And how I'd noticed that God never seems to repeat himself. If he offers a new opportunity it's always a new one, in a new way – never the old one again. And if somebody wants to be healed so they can go back to their old life, it never seems to happen that way either. If they are healed, it's so that God can offer them a new life, not their old one back again.

'So you couldn't pray for me, for the stoma to go now?' Amy said.

'I can only pray in the way God tells me to pray,' I said. 'And I haven't been told to pray for that one. Why don't you pray about it yourself, and ask him?'

'I don't know,' she said slowly. 'It doesn't feel right somehow.'

I remembered suddenly that she had prayed for something else, all those years ago. 'Do you remember saying to God that you'd do anything – even go through it all again yourself – as long as your children didn't get the same illness?'

She nodded. 'Do you think that's what happened?'

'I don't know. Do you?'

'I don't know.'

The sun was going down. It was getting cold.

'Oh well,' she said, getting up. 'No doubt we'll all understand everything eventually. When we get to heaven! In the meantime, we'll just have to make the best of it, I suppose!'

I suppose so.

10

CHAPTER

There were times when I felt the person who needed healing deserved more than being sent to someone God had asked to fail for him. So I took several people to other, well-known, ministers of healing.

With Michelle, the little handicapped girl from the children's home, I wrote to everyone I had ever heard of with a reputable (and successful!) healing ministry.

One wrote back and promised to pray for her, but said, 'You have the power to heal as well. Maybe the Lord wants to heal her through you.'

Another, at a local healing service, said, 'This child has had a lot of suffering,' at which point both Michelle and I began crying, followed by the two friends who had come to the service with us – so the priest prayed over all of us.

Then I took her to a religious community where healing services were held regularly. Michelle's parents were happy for her to go to these places, and we always asked them first, but they didn't want to go too.

I asked for the priest who had the longest-established record in healing ministry, and he came and prayed with Michelle. I was disappointed with the way he treated her. Although I told him she could understand things that were said, and was intelligent, he talked about her as though she wasn't there and made comments about her deformities that I felt were hurtful.

She was certainly very tense, and it didn't help when he slammed his briefcase shut right by her ear, and she jumped and began to cry. I could tell she didn't like him.

But he prayed, and at the end of the prayer he said to me, 'I don't know if you know it, but the Lord has given you a gift for healing as well, and I believe this child is meant to be healed through you.'

I took Michelle out into the garden. We had driven to the community's house with some friends, and they hadn't come out yet. I sat down under a tree with Michelle on my lap and gave her a drink, and apologized that the man had been a bit clumsy. I felt upset about it, and wished I hadn't brought her here.

Suddenly the air seemed to go still, as if time was suspended. It is never easy to describe these things, but it was another 'heaven come down to earth' feeling. Everything seemed to be holding its breath. I hadn't noticed how beautiful the garden was – the big old tree above us, with the breeze blowing through it.

I looked at Michelle, and saw that she was transfixed. Usually she sat with her head down, not focusing on anything, but her face was upturned, her mouth open, her eyes looking up towards the tree; her expression was that of someone paying rapt attention. She looked very happy. I felt very happy.

I realized then that it isn't very important if the people who minister healing are not very competent, or very sensitive, or fail to deliver the desired result. All they have to do is agree to be used by God, and God – who is the only source of health – will do his own healing, through them, in them and even at times despite them.

He is the one who heals. If one way is closed to him, he will find another one.

At that time, in the garden, it felt as though he was healing us both.

I went on going with Michelle to other ministers of healing. One service lasted three hours, but the atmosphere was low-key and comforting and Michelle was completely at ease. The priest prayed over her several times, and told me the Lord was using me as a channel of healing for her, but warned me not to take on the full responsibility for her.

At this time, the parents were suggesting that my husband and I fostered her, and they would have her for the occasional weekend, to give us a break. My husband felt it should be the other way round and had said, 'If we take on more responsibility for her, the parents will take less. I think you should stand back a bit and see if they'll do more.'

'What if they don't?' I'd said.

'That's a risk you have to take,' he'd said, 'for her sake.'

I felt he was right, and now this priest was confirming it. 'There are a lot of people carrying crosses that the Lord hasn't asked them to carry,' he told me. 'And the Lord is not asking you to carry this child yourself. Just pray for her. You have a life of your own.'

It was not long after this that the children's home Michelle lived in closed down, and the only place that could be found for her was a long way away. At the time, I was helping at healing services in a few parishes around where we live, and the man who was leading them also prayed with Michelle, and advised me, 'Maybe you and she have both achieved the Lord's purpose for you in each other's lives, and it's time for you both to move on now.'

I took Michelle out for a walk, before she left for her new home, and sat with her in the sun. I told her God had new work for us both to do, more things for us to learn and more growing up to do. He would always be with us, so we would never be alone. And we'd be with each other too, since he never brought people together in order to separate them. We were a good team and we would continue to be part of each other's lives.

She had done a good job with the people she had been living with in the children's home, and the people there – the children and the staff – were better for knowing her.

If ever she needed anything, I told her, she must tell God, and because she couldn't talk or speak up for herself, he would let somebody know she needed help. But she could also call on people herself, in her spirit, and there were people who would hear her. I told her I often knew when she was unhappy or needed help, and I'd pray for her.

But now there would be a difference. Now, if she was unhappy or homesick, she must call on her mummy. She would be the one now to tell. And although there had been times in the past when Michelle had cried for help and her mother hadn't responded, now her mother would hear her; she needed to hear her. It was time for them to get closer now, and it would work.

Michelle's mother had said recently that seeing all these people praying for Michelle and giving her all this attention had made her see Michelle as somebody special. She didn't know why, but she hadn't seen that before.

Michelle moved into the new children's home, and her parents visited regularly, and brought her home for visits. For her tenth birthday, because Michelle was frail and not expected to have the lifespan of other children, her family decided to give her the kind of party they would normally give a daughter for her eighteenth. They hired a hall and a disco and invited the whole extended family, the staff from her present and her previous children's homes, and friends.

There were family members there who had told Michelle's mother it would have been better if she had had an abortion, or if the child had died soon after birth. Some had never really seen her as a human being with her own personality or as someone with a life to lead, as valid as their own.

There were relatives and friends who had been afraid to hold her and had never had very much to do with her, because they were frightened of her frailty. And others had been afraid to get involved with the family because all they could see ahead was tragedy, and they felt unequal to the task of supporting Michelle's parents in all they had gone through and all they might still have to face.

But this evening they were all holding her and smiling at her and saying how lovely she was, and she was smiling back at everybody.

It was her party. And her triumph. She had done a terrific job of healing every one of the people the Lord had given her to help.

It's easy to forget that healing works both ways. Where healing is a profession – medicine or social work or psychotherapy, for example – there is a clear division between the person ministering and the person being ministered to: the professional and the patient.

It's not like that in Christian healing. God heals. We receive. He creates. We're created. He restores. We're restored. He's good. We're sinners being made good.

It sometimes seemed to me when I was laying hands on someone and praying with them that the wrong one was sitting in the chair, wanting healing, and the wrong one was standing over them, praying for them to be healed. People have asked me to pray over them when they are spiritually much healthier than me.

It's best to leave it to the Lord to decide. Sometimes I have said to him, 'Lord, this is the wrong way round!' and he's said, 'Leave it like this for now,' or, 'Let them decide. They find it easier this way.'

In the end, it doesn't make a lot of difference. Whichever one is doing the praying and whichever one is receiving, we both receive. I receive some of my healing through praying with them, and they receive some of their healing through me.

Sometimes, the Lord has reversed the situation. Someone has come for prayer and has ended up praying for me. A man came to the prayer group one evening and said he had the gift of healing. He was a mental patient, unemployed, and had been homeless. I was praying with people, but had to sit down and rest because I had bad stomach-ache.

He came over and said, 'Are you OK?'

'No,' I said.

'I can pray with you if you want. What's the problem?'

'My stomach. Thanks.'

He sat down and put his hand on my stomach. Several people rushed over to rescue me!

'He's praying with me,' I said.

He closed his eyes and prayed. The pain was replaced with a comfortable glowing warmth. He took his hand away.

'It's gone now,' he said.

'Yes, it has. Thanks.'

'I don't need paying,' he said.

'I don't get paid either,' I told him. 'Sad, isn't it?'

He started laughing. 'We'll get our reward in heaven,' he said, 'and not before bloody time either!' He shook hands with everybody and went to get a cup of tea.

On another occasion, a friend brought a young man called Fergus to the house. He thought he had AIDS. All the contacts he had had in the past two years had either been diagnosed as HIV-positive or had already died of the disease. He had become so afraid and depressed that he was in an almost catatonic state. He had been sitting alone at home staring at the wall for a couple of days, not sleeping, eating, or going out. His friend persuaded him to come and ask for prayer.

At the time, I had a slight problem of my own. I had had an operation six years previously. The stitches had been removed afterwards, all except one which seemed to be just below the skin. It was decided to leave it rather than try to take it out. The Sister explained that it would dissolve anyway within a few weeks.

After a few weeks, the piece of thread surfaced above the skin and came away. A while later, another piece appeared. The area around it looked slightly red. I asked the Lord what to do about it. He said, 'Leave it to me.' Another piece of thread appeared. I thought this was rather strange. If I pulled it, would yards of thread follow it? Would my insides unravel like a string vest?

I asked a nurse, who said that in the operation I'd had there would be layer upon layer of fine stitches internally, and stronger ones on the surface. The thread that had appeared was likely to be from a layer of internal stitching quite near the surface. But not to worry, she said. The thread was the kind that dissolved. It would take care of itself.

Six years later, there was still a hole through which a bit of stitch would appear every now and again. Now, in the past ten days, it had swollen into a red sore lump which was growing. Rapidly.

'Lord,' I reminded him.

'Leave it,' he said.

On the day Fergus came for prayer, the cyst – or whatever it was – was about the size of a tennis ball, and I had to cover it with cotton wool to keep my clothes from chafing it.

At first Fergus didn't talk at all. Then he said, 'I don't know if I want prayer. I've got nothing to live for anyway. I wish this disease would become active and I could get it over with.'

'What if God wants you to live? Would you give him the choice?'

He shrugged. 'I used to believe. But not any more.'

'He still believes in you.'

'Maybe. Maybe he wants me to have AIDS. Maybe I deserve it, I don't know. I haven't lived the way I should.'

I felt a wave of rage go over me. 'He doesn't want his children to be sick!'

'I don't know,' he said. 'How do you know? It could be my punishment.'

'*I* don't want you to have it!' I said. 'And he's nicer than me!'

He stared at me. 'Don't you? Why not?'

I don't quite know what happened at that point. The room went black and I could hardly see. It was like looking at him at the end of a long tunnel, and speaking from a long distance away. It felt weird, like the feeling you get before you faint. All the strength went out of me in one great whoosh! It was quite hard to speak.

'It's a horrible disease,' I said. 'I don't want you to have it.'

After what seemed like a long pause, he nodded.

The darkness cleared and the room looked normal.

'Ask him to heal you,' said the Lord clearly.

'What – now?'

'Yes.'

'Fergus,' I said, 'I've got this problem. I don't know if you can help.'

He looked surprised. 'What is it?'

'It's a cyst or something. Over an operation scar.'

'I'm a nurse,' he said. 'I could maybe see to it for you if I had a scalpel, but...'

'A scalpel! Thanks very much! I'm not asking to be stabbed. I want to ask you to pray with me.'

'I don't pray any more.'

'That's OK. Now is a good time to start. This thing is about the size of a tennis ball, hard as a rock, really sore, and I'm quite worried about it.'

'When was the operation?' he asked.

'Six years ago.'

'Six *years*! That's not normal. Not for a cyst to come up after all that time. You should go to Casualty.'

'I'm asking you.'

'I don't believe any more!' he said.

'I don't mind. You do the praying and I'll do the believing.'

He gave in. 'OK. Where is it?'

I pointed to an area of my abdomen. Quite low down.

'Oh no. Sorry. No offence,' he said, 'but you know I'm gay. I'm not at ease with women. Maybe if it was somewhere else...'

'I can't move it to some other part of the body you find more acceptable,' I said, 'and I'm not prepared to have a sex change.'

He laughed. 'OK. But... oh, OK. But nothing will happen, all right? I used to have faith and all that, but not any more.'

He pulled up a chair next to me, closed his eyes, and extended a hand gingerly in the direction of my stomach.

'Lord,' I prayed, 'if you want him back, get him now!'

After a second, Fergus stopped holding his breath and squeezing his eyes closed and started to pray. Really pray. I felt the effect. His friend looked at him, eyebrows raised. Something was going on.

Fergus sat back and let out a huge sigh. 'I'm exhausted,' he said.

'Thanks. I appreciate what you did.'

As he was leaving, he said, 'You shouldn't leave it, you know. Get it seen to at the hospital. Really.'

'I'll see how it goes,' I said.

Four days later, his friend phoned. 'Fergus wants to know if you've been to the hospital yet? He said it could be dangerous to leave that cyst.'

'Tell him no, I haven't. And if I look very carefully, I can just about see where it was. A very faint mark. And tell him God still believes in him, will you?'

I don't know where Fergus is now, but four years after I saw him he was in good health and good spirits, working full-time in a new job he liked: healing the sick.

11

When you think about it, the normal ways of loving people are fairly miraculous. Healing is commonplace. Every day, mothers heal their children. A child who has fallen over and cut herself risks infection. Shock doesn't help. A good hug relieves shock, builds up resistance and eases the healing of the wound. Nobody considers it a miracle.

We know how to heal – ourselves and each other. We've just lost faith in it. In God and in ourselves. It's safer to go to experts, even though we know mistakes can be made. At least they're not our mistakes!

Jesus said that the signs of being one of his followers were: proclaiming the good news (that we're forgiven and on good terms with God again), healing the sick, raising the dead, and casting out demons. Not signs of being a religious expert, or a religious fanatic. Just signs of being an ordinary one of his followers.

So why aren't we doing it?

Fear of failing?

But if he doesn't blame us for failing, what are we afraid of? Telling him we never even tried? Or didn't care enough that people were sick and frightened?

God can only work in ways that we accept and allow. So there may be someone who can only be healed through your prayer and no one else's. That person may only trust you. The fact that you feel embarrassed about offering to pray with them, or afraid of what they might say about you, is a risk, but it isn't the end of the world.

It can also be upsetting if the results are good! If you pray with somebody and feel a change occurring, and they get well right afterwards, their own embarrassment or fear of what people might think may make them disown it. So they say it was due to the new pills (even though they'd only taken one) or that they were never ill in the first place, or that it was a fluke. It's up to you then to thank God on their behalf. Later on, they may be able to.

But in the great scale of eternity, what people think about you is not going to be very important. Missing an opportunity to help someone cope with their life when they're struggling matters more in the long term. And you'll have loads of friends in heaven!

God works through everyone who is prepared to help, prepared to listen to him, and to let him stop them if they are getting it wrong.

You may not be the sole conveyor of his healing to someone, but an essential part of the team. If you don't do your part, you may be the 'missing link' that makes the difference between recovery or staying ill.

Sometimes people who seem to have no belief in God or his power to heal are delighted if you offer to pray with them. There have been several incidents which, for me, have confirmed what the Lord had said – that everybody knows him, at the deepest level of their being. There are times when someone seems to dip into that 'deepest level', right in the middle of a life which shows little or no awareness of God.

Samantha had a reputation as an 'enfant terrible'.

Despite the efforts of her quiet, respectable mother, she was always scruffily dressed with unwashed hair, scowling, and spitting in the street. As she grew up, she seemed to be on a campaign to shock the neighbours – having sex in doorways, running after any tradesmen who called to the street, and hanging around with gangs of lads drinking and plotting trouble.

Whenever I saw her on her way home from school and said hello, she would look up and answer with a surprisingly sweet smile. There seemed something really nice about her. But she had the air of someone who believed herself unlovable and had stopped caring what happened to her.

Her mother did care about her, and prayed for her every day. When Samantha found herself pregnant her mother was sad, though not surprised, and agreed to give her all the support she could.

After the baby was born, Samantha's mother said Sam had asked if I'd like to come and see her one day soon.

I called in and Sam showed me the baby, asleep in her cot. She was a lovely child, but lay very still. Something didn't look right.

'Is she OK?' I asked Sam.

'Really good,' she said. 'She sleeps right through the night – never wakes. But the health visitor says she shouldn't, at her age; she's too young. She says I should wake her up. But she seems all right.'

The child was perfectly formed with beautiful features. But her spirit seemed lifeless somehow – like the spirit of an old person who has become low and depressed. A newborn baby's spirit is usually bursting with life.

Sam asked if I wanted to hold her.

'She's sleeping,' I said.

'Doesn't matter. She sleeps all the time anyway.'

What went through my mind was 'cot death'. I started to pray.

'Lord?'

'Hold her against your heart,' he said.

I took the baby from Sam and held her with her heart against my heart. At once there was a great *thump* from my heart, so sudden and strong that it knocked the breath out of me. It felt as though jump leads had been attached to my heart and a great surge of power went out of it into the baby.

Immediately – although I'd only held the baby for a second – Sam said, 'Thanks,' and gave me a big smile, took the baby from me, put her back in her cot, and said, 'Sit down. I'll make you a cup of coffee.'

She put sugar in it without asking me, and I was glad of it. I felt a bit dizzy.

I was sure she knew that something had happened, and the moment it had been accomplished.

The baby is now a lively high-school student.

Something similar happened in a healing service in a local church: someone who had no experience of healing and no idea of what to expect seemed to know as soon as it was done.

An elderly man had come to the service, at the prompting of his wife. He had never been to one before, and was nervous. He was suffering from headaches, depression, and raised blood pressure that made him feel dizzy. When depression has failed to respond to any kind of treatment, there may be a spiritual element – a block of some kind that's preventing the flow of life and joy that can only come from God.

The man had been up to the altar for prayer from the healing minister, who sent him over to me to be prayed with some more. He didn't understand this.

'Why have I been sent over here?' he said. 'The others weren't.'

'He thinks you need a bit more prayer,' I explained. 'It saves you standing too long, if you come over here and sit down, and I can give you more time, without people getting impatient behind you in the queue. But if you don't want it, of course you don't have to.'

'Oh, well, I suppose. Go on, then,' he said grudgingly.

I began to pray with him and saw an image of demons coming out of him. This was obviously an image to help me. It's easier to know how to pray, and for how long, sometimes, if you have a visual aid!

These demons represented negative influences that were forming a 'mental block' in him and preventing him from experiencing freedom and joy. They were not very severe ones – things like cynicism, bad temper, and ingratitude – and he was letting them go. The prayer was soaking into him and he wasn't resisting God.

The trouble was, as they were released from him, he drew them back again. They were going, but not far enough away from him! It's not uncommon for someone to take back the very troubles they have let go; they're familiar, and it's easier to keep the status quo than to take on a new state of mind.

Still, he obviously needed a bit of help in giving them a real shove out of his life. The trouble was, it was the end of a long evening, we had been fasting since midday, and I was really tired. Every time I prayed, these demons came out – and he took them back again. I asked the Lord to help me.

Someone came up behind me, put their hand on my shoulder and started praying for me. Great. I knew it wasn't any of the people who usually prayed with me, because they were all involved in praying with other people, or hadn't been able to come tonight. But whoever it was was doing a good job. I felt some strength come back.

At the same time, the Lord said, 'Look up.' I looked up, and what I saw took my breath away. A huge angel, the height of the wall of the church, stood to one side of me. He looked like the angels in paintings, except there was nothing ethereal about him – he was solidly constructed, muscular and massive, and in his hands was a cricket bat, which I had certainly never seen in any paintings of angels! He held it up like a baseball bat, though, and as the demons came out from this man, one after the other he gave them a mighty swipe.

I watched this, open-mouthed, till the last one had been whammed into touch, to be dealt with, no doubt, by God. This was something!

But the next thing surprised me even more, if possible. The *exact second* the last of the man's problems had been dealt with in this decisive manner, and while I was still thinking, 'That seems to be the last one', the man stood up: the old man who had never been to a healing service and said he didn't really know what it was all about. He turned and said, 'Thank you very much,' brushed himself down and walked off. At the exact moment the healing was completed.

All that remained to do was thank the person who had come up from the congregation and stood behind me, praying for me. Their hand was still on my shoulder as I turned round to see who it was. But there was no one there. Or no one I could see, anyway!

It seems very clear to me now that a person's ability to receive healing from God is not at all dependent on knowledge, although many people place great store on understanding and search for spiritual enlightenment. It seems to have more to do with a pure spirit. If someone wants goodness, if they try to be loving, truthful, and not harm anybody, they are surely close to God, whether they know it or not.

Babies, who have come straight from God, are certainly close to him. Yet even among babies there are differences. Some are stronger in spirit than others. As an unborn baby absorbs nourishment from the body of its mother and can suffer if she is in poor health and benefit if she is healthy, so it seems that unborn babies soak up a great deal of the spiritual atmosphere around them. They can arrive in this world already spiritually well-nourished or undernourished, and the well-nourished ones obviously embark on life with an advantage.

We tend to think of unborn babies as not-quite human beings, yet in spiritual terms it seems to be the opposite. The spirit of an unborn child is as powerful as a nuclear generator! The fact that it is physically small or undeveloped has nothing to do with it. It is a tightly packed powerhouse of spiritual energy, joy, and enthusiasm. It would take a lot to dampen and suppress that life. Only look at the strength and determination of a child being born – fighting its way out into the world. Yet in physical terms, an unborn child is so fragile and dies so easily. I wonder how much it costs them to give up the life they have only just begun to embrace.

Courtney was in her twenties when a friend brought her to be prayed with, for depression. She had a live-in boyfriend and a little boy and said she should be happy but she wasn't. She had terrible nightmares every night, always the same one, and was afraid to go to sleep.

The dream was that she was holding a baby – a little girl, but her face looked just like her son's – and standing behind bars, in prison. On the other side of the bars was an old nun, reaching out her hands for the baby and saying, 'Give her to me. You don't deserve to have her, Courtney; you're not good enough.' And she pulled the child out of Courtney's hands, between the bars, and threw it on to a huge fire where it burned to death, screaming in agony.

While she was describing this recurring dream, Courtney was crying uncontrollably. I asked her if she knew what the dream was about; was there any connection with anything that had happened to her in reality?

She told me that last year she had become pregnant again. Her boyfriend said they couldn't afford another baby. He was planning a trip to Thailand next month with his mates and wasn't prepared to give up the holiday.

'What kind of holiday is it going to be?' I asked her.

'I don't know. He just said they were all going away together, him and his mates.'

'Whereabouts?'

'Bangkok, I think.' She was looking at the floor at this point.

'Is it a sex holiday?'

'I don't know. I didn't ask him.'

'A group of unmarried men, going to Bangkok together, a stag party? Did he ask you to go too?'

'No, he said I had to stay home and look after our little boy.'

'But it was because he wanted to go on this trip that he said you couldn't afford to keep the baby?'

She started to weep again. 'He said I had to have an abortion.'

'And did you?'

'Yes! I didn't have any choice. He said if I didn't, he'd leave me.'

'Do you think this is what your dream's about? The baby?'

'Yes,' she said. 'She looks just like my little boy. But in the dream the nun says I can't have another baby, because I'm no good. So she throws it away!'

It was a story I'd heard in different forms over and over again.

A woman – especially a young woman with a low opinion of her own value – in a relationship where she is not loved and valued as she should be, is told that her pregnancy is a problem. She may also have been led to believe, perhaps from childhood, that she herself is a problem. Becoming pregnant, with no means of support and a boyfriend who isn't prepared to put her or the baby first, is confirmation to her that she is a problem.

When abortion is offered, it's presented as the solution. By this time, the woman is seeing the baby as her problem and accepts the offer to terminate its life.

But the baby is not the problem. The problem is that the woman feels she has already been enough of a nuisance to everybody, and the least she can do is agree not to bring any more of herself into the world.

When the baby is gone, she still feels like a problem. The initial relief at losing the problem of the pregnancy is replaced before long by an awareness that she is still very unhappy – maybe more so than before – and feels even more valueless. It occurs to her that the baby might not have been the problem; the problem may be in her. The baby is no longer in her, but the unhappiness is. Then she feels even worse, because it wasn't the fault of the baby, who only wanted to live.

In addition to feeling she's no good at anything and no gift to anyone, she now feels she's no good to her own child either. She has let her own unborn baby be murdered. And the task of forgiving herself may be too much for her.

God doesn't blame. But he loves. He keeps loving the child whose life has been taken away, whom he always saw and still sees as a person with a life of its own. He loves the mother who was led to believe that her problem was being solved for her by the people who took the child out of her womb and left it to die.

And he loves the people who did it.

He doesn't reject any one of them. He is not into abortion. He sees value in everyone's life and rejects nobody.

But the same God who said, 'Thou shalt not kill' still means it – and means it kindly. It can never be a solution to a problem. It can only be a further problem, to add to all the ones we already have.

Still, death is not the end of anyone's story, and for Courtney's baby there was a further stage, and one that Courtney could help her with.

As she had seen the baby as a little girl, I asked if she would like to give her a name. She had already chosen one.

So we prayed together for the baby, by name, and baptized her in the name of Jesus Christ, and gave her back to the Father who had sent her here. We prayed for the baby to be comforted and healed of any sense of rejection by the world, and for the same for Courtney herself. Courtney told the baby she was welcome and she would see her later. They couldn't be together in this life, but they would be together in the Father's kingdom, and in the meantime God would look after them both.

Courtney cried all the way through the prayer, but afterwards she was calm, though very tired.

That was several years ago, and she had no more nightmares. She also gained the confidence to separate from her boyfriend, and is managing courageously to bring up her young son alone.

For Zena, the problem was a different one. She couldn't conceive. In her culture, childbearing was seen as a woman's whole purpose in life. Her sisters and sisters-in-law all had several children and planned to have more. They were a large family. Zena was the only one who had not 'fulfilled her purpose' in their view. They were very sorry for her, and one or two of her sisters-in-law had started treating her in a way that was patronizing, as though she were sub-standard, she thought.

Now even her husband, who had always been very supportive, was beginning to accept their condolences for him. She felt he agreed with them – that it was her fault and he had a raw deal in finding himself married to a dud wife who couldn't give him the children he wanted.

Although her situation seemed the opposite of Courtney's – who had conceived a child nobody welcomed – the root of the problem was the same. She felt valueless.

So first we prayed for her to realize her value to God – a value that wasn't dependent on her achieving anything, or producing children, or making her husband happy, but on simply being herself – the unique creature God had made and brought into the world, for his own purpose. And his purpose was for her to be happy. So we prayed for her happiness, whether or not she had a family of her own.

Then, there seemed to be some fear. The words of a psalm came to mind: 'I trusted, even when I said, "I am sorely afflicted," and when I said in alarm, "No one can be trusted."'

I prayed for her to be able to trust God, even when she felt she couldn't trust any other human being, not even the ones who loved her. And for her to forgive her husband, and for him to have the strength to bring his own grief to God, and not throw the weight of it on to his wife by making her feel responsible for his happiness.

Then I prayed for her to conceive, and to have not just one but as many babies as she and her husband could welcome and see as a gift.

She phoned up before two months had gone by. She was pregnant, and delighted, and her husband hadn't stopped hugging her all evening!

God does understand that not every child can be wanted. But he knows it's not the child that's the problem. The worry is that there won't be enough love to give the child, or enough time or enough energy or enough money. And there won't be – there never is, even if parents believe they are providing everything.

There are children from well-off backgrounds who are unhappy and lonely and frustrated and feel misunderstood and unloved. Their parents have tried to give them all the things that parents can give – and all the things that only God can give. But they can't, because they're not God. And a child who has been cut off from his or her creator is going to feel rootless, valueless, purposeless, and unloved.

God never wanted to have so little say in the welfare and upbringing of his children. After all, he gave them life. He wants to keep on giving it and being involved in it.

One extraordinary incident occurred with a mother who already had a large family. She managed very well, but she had had her last two babies in quick succession and was run-down and in poor health. Then Sara found she was pregnant again.

Her faith was strong, and she came round and asked me to pray with her, that she'd somehow find the love and enthusiasm to welcome this new child, and that God would give her strength to do all the work that had to be done even now, and the increase of work that would come with the new baby. She was trying hard not to cry as she said it.

I laid hands on her, and she did feel very weary and empty, as though the energy had been siphoned out of her and it was all she could do at the time to sit upright and listen to me praying.

I heard the Lord say, 'Ask her if she wants this child.'

I asked her, and Sara said, 'No, not really,' then burst into tears and said, 'I know that sounds awful, but I'm so tired, and I don't know where the money's going to come from!'

'Tell her,' said the same calm voice, 'that she doesn't have to have any child she doesn't want.'

I told her. Sara was horrified.

'Does that mean I've got to have an abortion?'

'Is that what you want?' I asked her.

'No! I've never believed in that! I think it's horrible!'

'That can't be what he means, then.'

'What does he mean?' she asked.

'I don't know. I suppose it means, leave it to him.'

'Maybe I'll have a miscarriage or something,' she said doubtfully. 'I don't like the idea of that either, though. It's not that I don't want the child...'

'I know. He knows. He's not blaming you. I think we'll just have to wait and see how it goes,' I said.

The time came for her to go to the hospital and have a scan. She was familiar with the routine, having been through it with all her other pregnancies. But on this occasion, it seemed to be taking a long time. The radiographer kept repeating the same moves.

'Is there anything wrong?' Sara asked her.

'Yes,' said the woman. 'I can't believe what I'm seeing.'

Sara had noticed that the woman had kept taking her glasses off and wiping them and putting them on again.

'What do you see?' Sara asked.

'There's definitely a pregnancy,' said the radiographer. 'There are all the signs of it. And the sac is intact; there hasn't been a rupture. You haven't miscarried. But there's no baby.'

'What do you mean?'

'I mean, it's just not there.'

'Is there any explanation why that would be?' asked Sara.

'Not that I know of. Do you?'

'Well, I did pray not to have the baby,' Sara told her, 'and I didn't want an abortion or a miscarriage. It looks like that's what's happened. It's gone.'

'Oh, praying wouldn't have anything to do with it,' said the woman quickly.

'Have you ever known it happen before?' asked Sara.

'Once,' she said. 'Last year.'

'What was the explanation then?'

'I don't know.'

'So it can happen,' she said. 'Without a miscarriage or an abortion.'

'I don't know.'

'Perhaps the other woman prayed as well,' Sara said.

I'm sure what happened to Sara wouldn't happen to every woman who felt unable to face her pregnancy. For me, the key factor was Sara's own faith. She was prepared to have the child. She was not prepared to make life easier for herself by taking the child's life away.

But she knew that she was going to have to rely on God for everything. She had none of her own resources left to care for another child – but she did want the child to be cared for. And she did know that God was the only one who could care for it as it needed to be cared for. What surprised her was that he cared enough about her, and her tiredness, to relieve her of the burden of another pregnancy in a way that neither she nor I could ever imagine.

This kindness by God increased her faith. By the time she got pregnant again, later on, she felt able to cope. If she couldn't, God would help.

But she wasn't prepared to hear the very disturbing results of her blood tests. They were repeated, and each time the result indicated an abnormality in the embryo – either Down's syndrome or spina bifida.

She was sent to a larger hospital for more sensitive tests. The baby was a boy, they told her, and they were sorry to say he definitely had spina bifida. Also, at twenty-two weeks, his head was too big, and lemon-shaped. Brain damage was indicated as well.

She was offered a termination, and rejected it. They asked her to reconsider. It would be difficult for her and possibly unfair on her husband and her other children, to have to spend so much time caring for a seriously handicapped child.

Sara came to the prayer meeting and asked for help. The whole group sat round her and prayed. She said afterwards that as soon as the prayer was over, she felt something change. She described it as, 'I felt my whole being filled with light.'

She and her husband prepared themselves for the arrival of their new son. They chose the name Joshua for him. Sara gave away all the girls' baby clothes and washed the boys' ones. This boy was to be their last child; they knew their limits.

When the baby was born, the midwife consulted Sara's notes and started laughing. 'This is the funniest boy I've ever seen!' she said.

The baby was a girl, perfectly formed, perfectly healthy.

'What happened to Joshua?' the other children wanted to know when they came to see their new sister.

But some questions only God can answer.

12

CHAPTER

Because God chose to heal one handicapped child, I thought it would mean he would always want to do that. But maybe the relevant factor was that the mother couldn't cope.

A mother brought her little girl to a healing service. The child was five and had Down's syndrome. When I sat down to talk to the mother, Gemma climbed on my lap immediately and gave me a hug and a big smile.

'I want to know if she can be healed,' her mother said.

'What of?' I asked.

'I want her to be normal.'

I laid hands on Gemma, who responded by winding her arms round my neck.

'Can she be healed, Lord?' I prayed.

'Of what?'

That was the trouble. There didn't seem to be anything wrong with her. Her spirit was alive, loving, warm, and bursting with joy and enthusiasm for life. Her face was one beaming smile.

I decided to hedge my bets. Perhaps there was something wrong with the mother, and the child was here to draw attention to her needs.

I asked if I could pray with Gemma's mother, and she

agreed. I prayed over her, but she seemed fine as well: a little bit lonely and anxious.

It struck me that they were a wonderfully healthy pair of souls. And a good team.

'Can you do anything for her?' she asked.

'I'm sorry,' I said, 'but I can't see anything wrong with her. She seems perfect. And you're OK too.'

'She can't become normal? I heard of somebody who had a miracle.'

'It happens sometimes, yes. But it seems to me that Gemma is here for you. She's come on earth for your sake – to help you.'

The mother looked puzzled. 'How can she help me?'

'It's hard to put into words,' I apologized. 'In her spirit, it seems that she's not separate from you. She doesn't want to be. She's part of your life and she wants to help you. She doesn't seem bothered about having a full life of her own. She likes being with you.'

The mother looked at Gemma doubtfully. Gemma threw herself at her mother, hugging her neck.

'She is very loving,' her mother admitted. 'So you can't heal her?'

'No.'

'Oh,' she said. 'OK.'

They walked out of the church hand in hand. They looked comfortable together.

Another non-problem the Lord saw no reason to heal was that of a lady who phoned to say she wanted healing because she was socially inadequate.

I had never met her, so I asked the Lord to show me something of who she was while we were talking. I couldn't see a problem, so I asked her why she saw herself as inadequate – who had told her this?

She said, 'My husband. He's very good at parties, but he says I slow him down. I sit there and say nothing, and he's fed up with it.'

'Do you ask him to take you home early? Is that what he's saying?'

'Oh no. I stay as long as he wants to.'

'Do you expect him to stay with you the whole time?'

'No, no. I do usually find someone to chat to. But sitting in a corner. He's out on the floor, the centre of things, and he says I should join in more. I cramp his style.'

'How do you cramp his style?' I felt there was something I was missing. I still couldn't see what she wanted to be healed of. 'You don't laugh at his jokes, or you look at your watch, or what?'

'No. I sit in a corner and have the odd chat with someone, or I have a drink and just watch.'

'Are you happy doing that?'

'Yes, I'm fine. But he doesn't like it. He's always the life and soul of the party, you see.'

Her husband was beginning to sound to me like a pain in the bum, but I didn't think it would be very Christian to say that. Or very helpful.

'What kind of social life do you have apart from parties?' I asked her. 'What do you like to do?'

'I have a few friends,' she said, 'but not many. We meet up for coffee.'

'One to one or all together, usually?'

'Usually one at a time. Maybe two or three once in a while. But never a whole crowd. We don't go out in a group. I don't have girls' nights out.'

Let me guess. 'And your husband says you should?'

'Yes. He has nights out with his mates and he says I should too.'

'Why?'

'I beg your pardon?' she said.

'God made you different from your husband,' I said. 'You don't have to be like him. You're fine being yourself. You have friends. People like you. You chat to people at parties who might otherwise be too shy to enjoy themselves. There isn't a problem, is there?'

'Are you saying you won't do anything to help me?'

'I'm saying you don't need help. You're fine.'

'But I'm not! I've just told you.'

It took quite a long time before she put down the phone. She was very disappointed I wouldn't pray for her to be healed to become like her husband, and she wanted her miracle. I did manage to refrain from saying I thought the miracle was that she put up with him. But on another occasion I didn't manage so well not to be rude.

I was at a weekday Mass and the priest called me into the house afterwards. He had a man in his office, making a routine enquiry about something, but the man had serious eye damage. While I was here, maybe I could pray with him to be healed?

I went in and met the man, who was grinning and making faces behind the priest's back. He obviously found the subject of healing prayer greatly amusing.

'Tell her what happened to you,' the priest invited him.

'I fell off my ladder at work,' the man said, still grinning, 'and cut my eye open. The hospital patched it up, and I'm off work, and the doctor told me not to move my head.'

He was looking back and forth between the priest and me as he said this.

'So what are you doing out?' I asked.

'I'm doing a bit of moonlighting. A friend gave me a few days' work.'

'Aren't you worried about your eye?'

'The doctor has told him he could lose the sight in that eye if he doesn't keep still and rest,' the priest said.

The man nodded his head up and down vigorously. 'That's right,' he said, laughing.

At this point, the priest was called out of the office to answer another phone.

'So,' the man said, 'you think I need healing, do you?' He looked me up and down and laughed.

'No, personally I think you need shooting,' I said, hoping the priest wouldn't come back just yet.

The smile dropped from his face.

'For taking a risk like that with your health,' I elaborated.

'I've got a family,' he said. 'I can't afford to lose work.'

'Can you afford to lose your sight?'

He was serious suddenly. 'No, I suppose not.'

'If I pray with you for the damage to heal up, will you do what the doctor says and go home afterwards?'

'I suppose I should,' he said.

'Well,' said the priest, coming back, 'have you prayed yet?'

'We're just about to,' I said. 'Right?' I asked the man.

'Right.'

His eye looked swollen and bloodshot. I asked him if it hurt.

'Yes.'

'Tell me if anything changes, will you?'

He looked sceptical but said nothing.

I prayed over his eye, and said, 'How does it feel?'

'Ice cold,' he said.

'Does that feel good or uncomfortable?'

'Good. A relief.'

I prayed for a few minutes longer and asked him how the pain was.

'Gone,' he said. He stood up, shook hands, and said, 'I'll go home and rest now for what's left of the day.'

It was normal for men to come for healing because their wife or girlfriend or the priest or some churchgoing friend believed. They were prepared to 'give it a try' but were inclined to be cynical, and were likely to brush it off as nothing if God did help them.

One man arrived at the end of a long day when I wasn't in the mood for comments about 'hands on' or having the 'magic touch' or any of the other phrases people use for reducing the healing power of God's love to a bar-room joke.

When he started saying he was only here because his wife had nagged him to come, and she believed in healing and such stuff, I interrupted and asked what was wrong with him. I knew his wife. She had had a long and painful history of gynaecological trouble and had recently come for prayer, mainly for emotional trauma resulting from the fairly gruesome treatment she had undergone in hospital. Hearing him laugh at his wife for believing fairy stories was painful. She was by no means a foolish or superstitious person.

He said he had bad backache and couldn't move. He turned sideways slightly and flinched. It had been like that for three weeks and was getting worse.

'And you don't believe God can heal people?' I asked. 'You're just here to humour your wife?'

'Well, and for myself,' he admitted. 'I'm willing to

give it a try. If the pain goes on like this I won't be able to go to work.'

'If I pray, and it shifts, will you believe me if I tell you what's wrong with it?' I asked him.

He thought about it. 'I suppose I'd have to, wouldn't I? If you could get it to go.'

The sore spots were not on the spine but on either side, low down. Over where the ovaries would be in a woman. Where his wife had most of her problems and pain. Was he taking on her pain and healing her? There certainly seemed to be nothing wrong with his back.

I laid hands on him, prayed for the pain and stiffness to lift, and felt heat go into him. I asked him how it felt.

'Like a radiator switched on,' he said. 'Heat going all through my back.'

'Can you move?'

As he had done before, he twisted from side to side. Then more vigorously. Then leaned forwards and back. Then bent down. Then wrenched his back fiercely backwards.

'Don't overdo it,' I said. 'Even for the sake of proving your wife wrong.'

He laughed. 'Go on then,' he said. 'What was wrong with it?'

'You're sure it's OK now?'

'Sure.'

'And you won't laugh?'

He grinned. 'I won't guarantee that! Go on, tell me. I can take it. What was wrong with me?'

'Congestion in the ovaries.'

'*What*?'

'You're healing your wife. Carrying some of the symptoms for her until she's strong enough not to get them any more. You've taken it on.'

His face was a picture. 'Is that normal?'

'It's voluntary. You offered. You told God you were willing to do it. It means you're a very good husband. You felt Karen had suffered enough.'

He wasn't joking any more. He said soberly, 'She has that. So there's nothing wrong with me, then?'

'Not a lot. But next time Karen's not well, pray for her. Then you might not take it on so much.'

'I can try,' he said. 'I'm not much of a one for praying, though.'

'You pray too hard, if anything,' I said. 'You really put your back into it! Let God take more of the strain.'

When I saw them again, he had given up his job and they had gone into business together and were doing well. A good team.

13

I was really beginning to believe now that God can't fail. And if someone wants God, and the health and peace that come with knowing him, they can't fail either. All they have to do is ask, and he will give them what they want – even if the whole world seems to be against them and they get crucified first.

It had begun to matter less to me whether the results of prayer looked successful. I was coming to accept what the Lord had told me at the very beginning: that the results were his business, not mine. My business was to pray, not to judge the outcome.

Without noticing the change, I had begun to take for granted the 'everyday' results of prayer: someone relieved of migraine, a high blood pressure returning to normal, a distressed baby suddenly peaceful. I was in the chemist's one day, and a young child sitting in a buggy was wailing and squirming about. Her mother was at the counter talking to the pharmacist.

I was feeling low at the time, and didn't want anything to do with it. I ignored the child. Her mother was obviously buying something to take away whatever symptoms she had, so why should I worry?

But the child reached out her hand and looked up. Her face was puffy and streaked with tears.

Reluctantly, I prayed, 'What's wrong, Lord?'

She was dehydrated, he said, and felt parched. She needed a long drink.

The mother looked very tired. I didn't feel like going up to her and saying, 'Your child needs a drink – now!'

So I took the child's hand and prayed for her to receive a flow of refreshment straight from God, and for her thirst to go. For inner coolness and calm.

The child kept holding my hand and looking at me. Peace fell. As on a few other occasions, it was a peace that could be felt – thick, like a blanket. The mother turned round and the pharmacist looked over.

'Well!' the mother said. 'You've certainly got the touch! You wouldn't like to come over and spend the afternoon, would you?'

'She might be thirsty,' I suggested.

'She could be,' she said. 'She's been sick a few times. I was up all night with her.'

I spoke to the baby. 'Mummy's going to take you home and give you a drink and a cuddle, and then you can both have a sleep!'

'Sounds like a good idea!' said the mother.

Where symptoms didn't evaporate, I learned not to panic or blame myself; just to accept the fact that the need was more complicated than it looked and might need more prayer over a longer time.

Often, one person's sickness highlighted needs in the whole family, and the 'sick one' turned out to be spiritually the healthiest, carrying the problems of the others. When other members started to acknowledge their own weakness, or to show symptoms of their own, the 'sick one' began to get well. If they carried on claiming to be spiritually healthy and believing their only problem was the sick person, the burden on the 'sick one' increased.

But I still found it hard to differentiate between success and failure in healing. God seemed to view it so differently.

I had thought that the first person who came to me for healing was a success. The results certainly encouraged me to go on. He came off drugs, healed relationships, and was quickly relieved of bad headaches.

His friend's healing was more of the two-steps-forward-one-step-back variety. He also came off drugs and drink and gave up one-night stands, but suffered a number of relapses in the process.

Yet the Lord said the first one was not healed, because spiritually he was not quite where he should be, given the amount of help he had received.

The second one, whose life still looked more chaotic, the Lord said was healed – 'because he loves me, and because he has forgiven you for the hard times he went through in changing his life and his attitude'.

There were still people who saw their successful healing as failures. Their symptoms may have been relieved, but they really wanted to be healed of being themselves, and were disappointed that they couldn't design who they wanted to be. When God heals, he only heals the person into being themselves more fully. This isn't good news for those who can't let go of the image they have of who they should be.

But there were others whose healing looked like failure, yet they saw it as a success and were content and praised God for it. One of those was Elise.

I met Elise through a friend who had very strong faith and had encouraged a lot of people to start to believe, or return to believing, in Jesus. Elise was one of them. This friend didn't see healing as part of what God was calling him to do at that time, so when Elise was in trouble he invited me over to pray with her, and I went with a friend from the prayer group.

Elise had been going through a period of confusion, torn between her faith as a Christian and her live-in relationship with her boyfriend. Clearly, in terms of Christ's teaching, she couldn't both follow him and continue to sleep with a man who wasn't her husband. Now she was pregnant, and the situation was more complicated.

She was expecting twins, a boy and a girl, and the scan had showed that one of them was very sickly, with a serious heart defect. She had been warned at the hospital that this child was unlikely to survive the full term of the pregnancy, and that if she miscarried, the healthy twin was likely to be lost as well. So she wanted us to pray that the healthy child would survive, and if possible the sick one would be healed.

Her own faith was strong and her character was open. She was ready to receive what God wanted to give. But she also had a very strong sense of guilt and unworthiness, which seemed to be reflected in the girl child – the sick one.

Her boyfriend was committed to the relationship and willing to support her and the twins. He wasn't a Christian, and within his own morality was doing the best he could, Elise said. He wasn't the one she blamed for the relationship going as far as it had without leading to marriage. She blamed herself. Also, she wasn't sure he was the right person for her to marry, and she felt guilty about that as well, when he was so concerned about doing his best for them.

This seemed to be where the problem was. Elise loved God, but she couldn't believe he would forgive her and want her to have nothing but happiness, at least until she had 'put the situation right'. But it was hard for her to know what was best, in the present circumstances – and they were beyond her power to arrange differently now. She would have to rely on God to bring goodness out of the situation as it was, rather than trying to make good what had gone awry.

The Lord had told me at one time that the way a person treats their child reflects the way they treat their soul. Often, a person with no conscious faith in God would change when they had a child of their own: they would re-write their priorities and change their view of life, now that they had a child to take care of. And that was their opportunity to learn to take care of their soul. In fact, he sometimes used the words 'child' and 'soul' interchangeably.

So I could see how important it was for Elise to accept that God would heal her soul if she asked him, regardless of what she had done or how complex the circumstances she now found herself in.

In praying for the little girl to grow strong and healthy, it was essential for Elise to allow her soul to be soothed by God's forgiveness. But when I prayed for this, her spirit seemed to shy away from accepting it, almost as if she believed she would only feel better if she was punished.

At the same time, I felt that the friend praying for Elise with me had something of the same attitude. Until then we were praying in unison and her prayer was definitely reinforcing my own: two souls were better than one! But at the point of praying for Elise to have every one of God's blessings, there was a withdrawal.

I began to pray for the friend as well, but it was as though her spirit shied away from the same thing: she felt unworthy, unclean, and in need of punishment. In this respect, her spirit was agreeing with Elise's own doubt and reinforcing it.

I tried to leave her to God and concentrate on Elise, but it wasn't easy to do this. In some ways, she seemed to be in more need. Her spirit was crying for help, but then she was telling herself she didn't need it; she was all right.

I finished praying, and could only hope that the baby had absorbed enough of the prayer to be healed.

The friend who had introduced me to Elise phoned me after the birth. Both babies had been born safely, but the little girl had died shortly afterwards.

I was devastated to hear this, and wrote to Elise to offer condolences for the death of her little girl, and to wish her every blessing on the birth of the little boy.

Far from seeing the prayer as a failure, though, Elise was very happy. She phoned me and said, 'I never expected the little girl to live; she was just too sick. But I thought I'd lose my son as well, and here he is. You have to come and see him: he's so beautiful!'

And he was, a lovely little boy with a warm and open spirit. After I had seen him, I had to agree with Elise and stop seeing the prayer as a failure. That it could have been better, more complete, I didn't doubt. But Elise was happy, and ready to tackle the issues involved in sorting out her relationship with her boyfriend and committing herself more fully to God. Even a partial healing was not to be despised.

It worried me, though, that a problem in the person

who prayed could prove a block to the person who needed to be healed. That person needed help in removing their own spiritual block against allowing God's love to flood every corner of their lives. To be able to help shift some blocks while leaving or even reinforcing others, seemed very sad. And surely my spirit was lacking in this area: I had prayed against this double dose of guilt, Elise's and my friend's, and hadn't had enough faith to shift it, which suggested to me that I was not strong enough either in this area of accepting forgiveness.

I would almost have preferred not to pray with anyone at all than to have such a patchy effect. But that was pride. Repeatedly, the Lord told me not to wait till I was perfect or felt I had something to offer: I would surely wait a long time, and so would everybody else! I was just to pray, and leave the results to him, including the results he would produce in me. In praying for others' healing, I was also being healed – slowly, uncertainly, two steps forward and one step back at times, but inevitably. I had to be content with that.

In my own life, there were some testing times ahead. My family had its share of divisions and prejudices and at times it seemed as though history was destined to go on repeating itself indefinitely and that some attitudes would never change.

But the Lord hadn't finished with us yet.

One lesson he had for me centred around an issue that causes trouble in many families, and that so many people find a stumbling block in their relationship with God: money.

14

CHAPTER

A member of the 'rich side of the family' (I grew up on the 'poor side'!) had a birthday and invited me. A meal in a very plush hotel; carpets so thick you bounced as you walked on them; crystal chandeliers; tables draped in white damask, miles apart; fountains in the middle of the restaurant, falling into an artificial stream the whole length of the room, with fish swimming in it.

Waiters bowed as they showed us to our table (reserved weeks in advance). The concierge who welcomed us waved us towards another one in the hall, who deftly removed our coats and whisked them away to spend the evening in a perfumed sanctuary, in the company of yet another member of staff. (My companions' coats were fur and soft leather; mine was a mac from C&A's sale, but the atmosphere was so hallowed that everyone pretended not to notice).

We were ushered into padded chairs and had white napkins, starched like boards, waved on to our laps. The waiters whirled and glided around us like skaters. Menus were presented with a flourish, opened ready for us to read, to save us the faintest effort. The names of the dishes were in several languages. The prices were in Monopoly currency.

At this point, my appetite vanished. I'm not good at

maths. I struggled to convert those prices to sterling, and then to reality. Surely they couldn't be that much. Not for a *meal*. The price of a starter portion would have kept an Indian village in rice for weeks.

'Lord,' I said inwardly, 'a third of the world is starving. I can't eat here. I don't want to hurt anyone's feelings, so give me some way to leave without causing offence.'

Sometimes the voice of God comes very quietly. I worry, 'Was that really his answer? Or just my own ideas?'

This time it was loud and firm. 'Stay. Celebrate the birthday – in their way, not yours.'

I stayed. It was really hard.

I wasn't paying, but I couldn't help thinking that the starving rest of the world was.

I asked my relatives to order for me; I'd have what they had.

It all tasted very nice, but every mouthful would have paid for a meal for several people.

I thought of one-parent families living on tower block estates, on Income Support; of beggars in Bombay. To my right, under the fountain, swam overfed fish. A lady in evening dress, dining alone, called the waiter and requested a special dish not on the menu. He acquiesced graciously, bowing away.

A well-dressed family came in, towing two sullen adolescents reluctantly dressed in smart 'respectable' clothes.

Seeing them brought back memories. I remembered another dinner in a hotel, hosted by wealthy members of the other side of the family, during my own adolescence.

My mother had issued anxious instructions on etiquette before we met them: elbows off the table; start

with the outside set of cutlery and work in; don't say if
you don't like something, just leave it discreetly on the
side of the plate. She worried about whether my sister
and I had 'proper dresses' to wear; clean shoes; newly
washed hair; clean handkerchief (not to be used at table);
polite smiles; small talk; gratitude for the favour of being
included in this occasion. I can't remember what the
occasion was.

I do remember some of the conversation at table.

'Larry's a fool – living on his capital. If you can't live
off the interest, you shouldn't retire.'

'My stockbroker recommended buying shares in
Blonks, but I decided to buy more of Blinks instead, and
they're doing quite well.'

'How are your investments doing?'

'Have you had your trip to Canada yet this year?'

'Arnold and Sally have seen a house they like. But only
a hundred-foot garden, so they'll have to keep on looking.'

My mother and sister and I were living on social
security, trying not to grow out of our shoes. A few times,
we ran out of money to buy sanitary towels. That was the
worst. Degrading. Now we were expected to sit smiling
while our relatives provided one meal in a hotel and two
hours of conversation about the problems of investing
and multiplying their surplus thousands.

I began to recognize that my discomfort here tonight
as an adult, in this other hotel, had as much to do with
the past as with the present. But the relatives who had
invited us to that meal had all died now, and I had to let
the past go.

Granted, it had hurt that they hadn't helped when we
needed help. They had called it 'being responsible' to
protect their investments, but hadn't felt any

responsibility for their own family in difficulties ('After all, it's not as if they are *immediate* family'). And it wasn't my responsibility to ensure that their actions in the past had no lasting effect on me. We all carry our own history with us and if it didn't affect us, or we let ourselves forget, we'd never learn anything.

But they were gone and I had to banish their ghosts, and not allow the memory to overshadow the birthday of another relative now.

That they hadn't been able to let go was their tragedy. A part of their hearts had got locked up in the bank vaults along with their money. But if I couldn't let go of what they had done, or hadn't done, then that would be my tragedy. We'd survived. The only way I could lose out now was by bitterness over that history, which had possibly taught me some things of value.

I had a choice: to concentrate on the well-cooked food and the smiling faces and enjoy the company now, or to keep the bitter taste of the past in my mouth and let it sour the flavour of both the present and the future.

The reflection of the chandeliers blended with the twisting glint of the fish in the water. Music wrapped itself smoothly around the tables, insubstantial as air, too discreet to be tuneful. Reality and unreality melted boundaries. The past and the present blurred.

'A little more, Madame?' The waiter already had the silver ladle poised above my plate.

'Non. Merci.'

He didn't take my refusal seriously. 'Just a little more of the sauce.'

Never finish eating before everyone else. Another of my mother's instructions. Just push the last few forkfuls around the plate. Pretend to be still eating. Or take a little more of the sauce. Otherwise those who are still eating may feel uncomfortable – greedy, even. Don't let anyone feel uncomfortable, at any price.

But I was uncomfortable and didn't know how to cope with it. Overfull, even though I had asked for only a tiny portion, pleading a small appetite.

The others hadn't finished eating. The waiter lowered the ladle over my plate.

'*Non!*'

He looked at me, startled, and withdrew quickly.

I looked at my empty plate. I wanted to do what the Lord was telling me. Celebrate. Regard it as a Eucharist. But it seemed too much to swallow. The events of the past had been a lot to swallow, but I'd thought the past was finished with, long ago now. But here it was back again suddenly, and it stuck in my throat. I felt thirteen years old, instead of thirty or so.

I wanted to cry.

I wanted to go home and be in the garden, in the fresh air (even though our garden was nowhere near the hundred-foot-long one despised as too small at that other dinner party).

I had just consumed the equivalent of a whole family's meal, in financial terms. It could have been my own family's, some years ago. And all these well-dressed people still didn't care.

'You can do it. Stay. For me.'

It was the Lord all right. The same voice as usual. The same calm, gentle, loving, sure serenity. Telling me to sit here, be here, share in the meal, smile, raise the heavy crystal glass and drink a toast to the birthday.

'Their way of celebrating, not yours. Do it their way. For me. For love.'

I knew it was him, then. He'd said the same thing to me before.

'Look at the people. Don't look at people and see money. Look at the love.'

I looked at the people sitting opposite me. They needed this. I needed it as well. To celebrate life, and the passing of years, and being together – being a family.

A strange family; unequal; alienated from each other and the way that the others lived. Perhaps unable to imagine the reality of being poor, day by day. Perhaps afraid. Perhaps uncaring.

But ready to share this, anyway. Offering the best they had on this occasion.

And was I going to refuse it, because of what hadn't been offered on other occasions when it was needed more?

Their problem was that they hadn't been able to give. Was mine that I couldn't receive, even when they did get the hang of it?

The solution to inequality seems so obvious, doesn't it? Yet if families find it so impossible to envisage sharing what they have among themselves, no wonder we find it inconceivable on a global level.

We look at the imbalances in the world – the small group of friends who dined out and spent over £3,000 on a bottle of wine with their meal. The young woman lying in the street in Bangalore, with her baby waving the flies away from her face and still trying to feed from her empty breasts, not realizing she was dead. The family who can't pay their rent *and* buy the groceries and have to choose between the two.

The solution screams at us. Screams at God.

What do we do with the anger? Doesn't God have anger? What about justice?

But I'm rich too. We have a car, a computer, a microwave, holidays, plenty of clothes, the freshest food of the season – raspberries, new potatoes, fresh fish and meat.

Who am I depriving? Am I depriving anybody? Or is there really enough for everyone, as long as we do our sums God's way and don't look at our lives in isolation from – or in competition with – anyone else's?

'Look at the people. Don't look and see money. Look with love, and see the need for love, the need for joy. They're trying so hard to find it in all these things they accumulate, because they've forgotten how to find me.'

'Lord, do you want me to give away all I have, then? Jesus, what you said to the rich young man – "Sell all you have, give the money to the poor and come follow me" – is that what you're saying to us all? Or are there some things we're meant to keep? To receive gratefully? To be ready to part with them gracefully as well, but only if you say so? Teach me. Let me see as you see.'

'Know the value of money, that's all. Know the value of people.

'Money has no value, on its own.

'I'm your Father. Sometimes I like to give you a treat. What's wrong with that, I ask you? I didn't come to preach austerity.

'Does the creator of the universe believe in keeping things small? The creator of abundant life, a million varieties of every species – do I want you to live a dull life? Afraid to enjoy, afraid to receive, afraid to provide and be provided for?

'Afraid to give?

'Afraid to let go?

'Afraid of losing out, letting someone else win?

'No.

'You can't ask too much of me. I have everything to give you all.

'But, if you really are looking for the giver, don't look too long at the gifts. They only exist to lead you to me.

'If they led you away from me, why would you want those things? What value would they have? Less than nothing.

'So whether you give or receive, do it for me. Do it with love. With my blessing.

'And never give anything to anyone, unless you are prepared to give it to me.

'That way, you're never rejected, even if the person you give to rejects your gift. Even if they waste it, or use it to ruin their life, or throw it away.

'Love is never wasted. It never ruins. Only bitterness can do that to you.

'Don't be angry, if you give away all you have, and the person who receives it considers it nothing.

'It doesn't mean nothing to me. I know what it cost you. It cost a lot of love. Don't take back the love if the gift gets thrown away, or the receiver doesn't know how to use it for good. Just come to me. I can forgive them for you. I can give them my blessing. I will teach them, eventually, how to value my gifts. Don't strain to do any of these things yourself. They may be beyond you, just yet. Don't be like a child who keeps struggling to tie her own shoelaces, refusing help, while you still can't see why it won't work out for you.

'Let me handle this my way for now.

'Stop trying to work all this out, with a tired mind.

'You will understand, I promise.

'This is still my world. I have put it into the hands of humankind for a while.

'Why?

'Because you do know, deep down, how it works. Everyone does understand really. You know your own part in this world, and how to live. You know that kindness works miracles and bitterness kills.

'But there's so much noise and you consume life with such intensity. So much to distract your attention and divert your consciousness.

'Slow down. Be still for a while. Listen.

'I am still God. I haven't forgotten how.'

The meal in the hotel turned out as it was meant to be – a family celebration, God's way: the way of allowing us choice and asking us to respect others' choices. And perhaps because it was done his way, by the end of the evening it did feel like a celebration, a memorable chapter in a family history that was uneven and imperfect, but from which God was never really absent.

15

Filtering out false ideas is part of everyone's healing. It's worth doing the occasional stock-check on what you believe and seeing where those beliefs have come from, whether they are really what you think, or just what the people around you find acceptable. Some ideas are plausible, pragmatic, and practical, but not actually true.

When prayers don't get answered, it's time for more questions. I have often found I am praying for two different things at once. I'm asking God to give me something that I secretly have a few doubts about. Or I'm asking for only a half-remedy to a problem that needs a more sweeping solution.

Jesus said, when criticized for the way he lived, 'I can only do what I see the Father doing.'

We can all probably only do what we see our god doing – which calls into question who our god is. The one who gave us the Ten Commandments as a recipe for a human and happy life, or the god of success and achievement, or the god of approval and pleasing everyone?

A parent who was having trouble with her teenage son was expecting him to live according to her rules of life, and was very frustrated to find that his view was different. As far as he was concerned, he was leading a very good life, living up to *his* commandments. And he didn't think much of her gods. At seventeen, his personal Ten Commandments went something like this:

Don't grass on your mates.

By the time you're seventeen you must have got: a tattoo, laid by at least six different girls, a driving licence, and a fake over-18 ID card to use in nightclubs.

Clothes must be designer-label cool: jeans must be button-fly not zip-front; boxer shorts must be Calvin Kleins; soles of trainers must be no less than 6 cm thick.

Get as much money as possible, by any means possible: nicking car radios, bullying parents, pushing drugs or, if all else fails, working.

Don't do a job that marks you out as boring.

You're a saddo if you stay home on a Friday or Saturday night.

You're nobody if you haven't got wheels – a car or, better still, a motorbike.

Don't ever get seen buying tapes instead of CDs, however broke you might be.

You must have been to the States at least once by the time you're nineteen.

Do not, at all costs, grow up to be like your parents.

Quite a harsh religion. It would require a lot of vigilance and anxiety to keep all those rules and fulfil all those aims. The added difficulty of course was that he had to live with people who didn't belong to the same religion and who insisted that he complied with their rules, not his.

So he had a double risk of failure. If he failed to practise his own religion, he faced certain punishment:

he would lose respect from his mates and the guys considered cool on the streets and in the clubs.

If he kept his own rules but failed to keep society's or his parents', he also faced punishment: he wouldn't be allowed to borrow the car, be given some of their money, or go out on Saturday night.

In addition, if he went too far in his own religion, he could be arrested and get a criminal record. He was aware of these risks, but didn't believe it was fair or democratic to be persecuted for his religion.

However, he couldn't escape the morality of his society, community, and family. The things he was told were wrong when he was a child at home or at school remained in his system even if his conscious mind chose to reject them. As time goes on and he grows older, they may rise to the surface again.

He may no longer be so confident that his religion is the only one worth belonging to. Other people's religions may seem to have something valid to say.

This causes confusion. If morality is not so cut and dried – not 'My rules are real life; yours are just nitpicking' – then the occasions for guilt multiply, and guilt is a form of discomfort that nobody likes.

What is your religion? Not the official one you write on forms that ask you to state your religion, but the motley collection of teachings from childhood, peer groups, society, and the currently fashionable political or media figures?

You may not like, or believe in, the set of rules that make up your own personal religion. But every now and again it demonstrates its hold on you, influencing your decisions, making you do things you don't want to do and evade things you do want to do.

What are the Ten Commandments that lurk in the back of your mind and make you feel guilty whenever you break one of them?

My unwritten (and unchosen, and unwelcome) Ten Commandments might go something like this:

Thou shalt work hard, take it seriously, and not enjoy it. Writing books – especially novels – is not proper work, so anything serious and unenjoyable must take precedence over it and anyone who does 'real work' is entitled to interrupt it at any time.

Women's lives shall be fulfilled by either having children or having a full-time (serious work) career, or both.

Thou shalt not go out until thou hast finished the ironing.

Don't be one of those idle and unproductive people who waste an entire week of holiday lying on the beach, and don't you know you're far too old to jet-ski? Cultured adult people go sightseeing and come home with guidebooks and sunstroke to show for it.

Don't be one of those *extremely* idle and unproductive people who sunbathe in the back garden on a weekday when real workers are in offices; writing the final chapter of your book at midnight instead doesn't compensate for it.

Thou shalt consume alcohol in large quantities at parties or else be considered boring and unable to enjoy yourself.

Thou shalt not want to go home after an hour at even a really great party unless you want to be considered boring and socially disabled.

It is not permissible, in company with other women

sharing fantasies about male Hollywood idols, to say you think they look constipated and could be sulky in the mornings.

It is not permissible, in discussion with other women about ordinary men and their general hopelessness, to confess that your husband is not particularly annoying/selfish/untalented/undesirable/insanitary or useless around the house, and you actually quite like him.

Thou shalt not mention God as a person you admire and like, rather than as an abstract concept to be dissected by all self-respecting intellectuals. If you do you may confidently expect to be ostracized from all social life.

Now, these commandments should never cause me to feel any guilt at all, however frequently I break them, because I don't believe any of them. Also, of course, they are mainly so trivial that it makes very little difference whether they are kept or not.

The problem comes when I have them in the back of my mind, and also try to keep in mind the Ten Commandments, or their succinct summary by Jesus Christ: Love God with your whole heart, soul, mind and energy, and love your neighbour as yourself.

When two sets of commandments conflict, they can't both be from God. If one god makes the decision ('Ironing is necessary and also tedious so must therefore have more value than going for a walk and ending up having a chat with the *Big Issue* seller in the shopping precinct'), then I am not giving the real God any choice. My spirit is silenced, because I am on autopilot. I'm acting on some instruction, having forgotten where it originally came from and why I'm still allowing it to influence me.

I really don't know where I got my hang-up about work having to be a drag or else it's not real work. What I do know is that it's one of the unconscious ideas that can still interfere with the steering system I've consciously chosen to guide my life.

If I want to override it and prevent it from still having an influence then I have to be sure of what my steering system is, and remember to keep it switched on.

My chosen steering system is the Ten Commandments given to Moses by God, and endorsed wholeheartedly by Jesus Christ. Because they're brilliant. They cover everything and they're permanently relevant, since human beings haven't really changed their nature since the moment of being created (either instantly or as a gradual evolution – does it matter really, since we all have a moment of creation and we're all still evolving?).

Because these are the guidelines I choose to live by, I don't want to get sidetracked by issues that aren't moral at all, or relevant to eternity – commandments such as 'Thou shalt not eat chocolate,' or 'You're a disgrace to womanhood if your weight goes above ten stone.'

If you'll excuse me for being gruesome, it's a sobering thought that if we are overweight now, the weight is going to just fall off us – the minute we're dead. And our spirit will weigh less than nothing. So while I'm here, I can be as solid or as skinny as I like, as long as I keep my spirit light – keep being carried along by God's way of living life.

APPENDIX TO
CHAPTER 15

Ten useful commandments (yes, the original ten) in contemporary language:

I am God, the only one. Don't create other gods, goals, idols, moralities, or philosophies and give them priority over me. Remember, I've brought you to this point in your history and only I can lead you beyond it.

Don't use my name abusively, or use me to justify your abusive thoughts or words or actions against human beings.

Keep a day of peace in your week: time set apart to be aware of God – for you and for your family, children, servants, lodgers, or visitors in your home. (And watch this space to see how that period of awareness and peace overflows into the rest of your week!)

Respect your father and mother; don't put them on a pedestal as though they were perfect and then knock them off it because you're disappointed they're not; respect their reality – the good, the bad, and the ugly – as human beings.

Don't kill anyone; don't write them off in your mind; don't deprive anyone, in any state, of their right to their own life.

Don't commit adultery; that is, don't adulterate good relationships with the confusion, contempt, and hurry, of lust.

Don't steal – anything, from anyone, including big faceless organizations; don't steal anyone's time by using them as company in 'killing time'.

Don't gossip or spread rumours or lies about anybody; don't be an audience for gossip, lies, or rumours either – however fascinating.

Don't lust after someone else's wife/husband/ partner; keep your mind on your own if you have one, or else be content with your singleness for the time being.

Don't envy someone else's possessions, achievement record, appearance or fame; be thankful for your own, even if what you have seems to you to be less desirable and impressive.

(You can add more commandments here of your own – but who needs them? These are quite enough of a challenge to be going on with!)

16

Casting out demons is on the same lines as filtering out false ideas. A person may do this for themselves, or they may need a little help. Or, if those ideas have completely swamped their personality and distorted their reality, they may need God to be involved in a major way, to move in on their life with a firm hand.

But however 'out of their mind' they may be, their spirit still needs to agree to let God act. At some level, even if in a tiny way, they need to say yes to God and no to their demons.

We use the expression that someone is 'fighting their demons' when they are in a state of turmoil that prevents them from continuing with their normal everyday life – an ex-soldier, for example, plagued with flashbacks to scenes of terrifying violence.

Our 'demons' vary, but are uniformly destructive to our reality as human beings. Demons are like old socks: if they're not thrown out, or put through a boiling hot wash, they will stink the whole room out. A life which harbours even one little demon is not going, in the long run, to be a wholesome life.

So how does anyone go about getting rid of the old smelly socks that swamp the fresh air and perfume of the rest of their life?

They make a choice. Simple as that. Even if they're not strong enough to carry it out by themselves. They choose to live a good life – even if it means throwing out some well-loved idea that has been part of their life for so long that they feel their whole identity is wrapped up in it.

And then they give God permission to go into their room and chuck out the dirty laundry. And let him decide what's to go and what's to stay, and what they still need to acquire.

Annette was a fairly recent member of the prayer group I used to attend. After a meeting one week, she followed me out to the car and asked if I would give her a lift home.

I apologized and said I couldn't: I had a car full of people to drive home already, all in the other direction; the petrol tank was nearly empty and I had no money on me to buy more, even if there had been a petrol station still open at that time of night. It had been a late finish that evening.

Good reasons for saying no, and plenty of them. But she kept insisting. She didn't want to go back to the meeting room and ask if there was anyone else who could drive her home. She didn't want me to ask for her. She would wait till I returned from taking the other people. She didn't listen when I said there wasn't enough petrol.

'Say yes,' the Lord instructed.

I said yes. Not very politely.

When I picked her up, she told me where she lived. It was a couple of miles away, in an area I didn't know. I have poor night vision, which makes it unsafe to drive after dark, and the area wasn't well-lit. I also have a lousy sense of direction, and wasn't at all sure I could find my way home.

'Don't worry,' the Lord said calmly. 'What you're really worried about is that she's going to lead you into an area where you'll get lost and won't be able to find your way home. But I'll get you home again. Trust me.'

By then, I really didn't have much choice.

As soon as I started driving, Annette told me she had a problem. A spirit had taken over her mind and she kept hearing a voice telling her to do things. She had phoned the bishop and said she felt she needed exorcism. He had told her to speak to the priest and ask him to pray with her, and she had done that, and felt calmer after the prayer, but the spirit was still with her.

She had phoned the bishop again, and he said he would pray about it and she should call him back next week, when he would let her know the outcome of his prayer for her. If necessary, she could have an appointment with the exorcist (every Catholic diocese in the UK has a priest who fulfils this role), but he hoped it would not be necessary.

She asked me if I would pray for her.

I asked what this spirit was and what kind of trouble it was causing her. She said the form it took was of a man who had died young, who was in love with her. The trouble was, it sounded exactly like the kind of person she would like to meet. He had described himself and was just her type. But he kept on telling her to do things, and although so far they had been pretty harmless, she was afraid that might change.

'Have you tried saying no?' I asked.

'Oh yes, but it's quite unusual, what's happening to me, isn't it?' she said. 'I mean, why should I be picked and not someone else?'

I took my eyes off the dark road and looked at her.

There was a glint of excitement in her eyes.

'It's not unusual,' I said. 'It's quite a common nuisance. You deal with it like any other nuisance – like a bore at a party who won't leave you alone. This is the supernatural equivalent of the bore at the party. You tell it to go away and stop bothering you.'

She didn't answer. I realized she was quite a shy person and might never have had the experience of someone at a party demanding her phone number.

'It's not exciting,' I said. 'Is it?'

'Well, no,' she said. 'But it is different, isn't it?'

'Have you ever been involved in anything occult?' I asked her. 'Spiritualist meetings, seances, fortune-telling, astrology, tarot, that kind of stuff?'

'The bishop asked me that,' she said. 'No. I'd be afraid of that kind of thing. Why do you ask?'

'Evil requires a loophole. You have to leave a door ajar in your spirit for it to get in. If you haven't gone looking for something supernatural, though, it could just be that you're vulnerable. Have you been chucked by a boyfriend or something, recently?'

'No.'

'Could you be lonely?'

There was a hesitation, then she said, 'Could be. This man, though – I mean, I could relate to somebody like that. Maybe we were destined to be together. If he hadn't died young.'

'It's not a man,' I said. 'It's a voice inside your head. Restricting your freedom, because you can't hear yourself think.'

'But he *was* a real person,' she insisted. 'He even told me where he used to work.'

When I didn't say anything, she said, 'You don't

believe he ever existed, do you?'

'No,' I said, 'but it doesn't make much difference. It's either a distraction, taking the form of a person you're likely to find attractive, or else it was a real person once but now he's dead. Either way, get him out of your head and get on with your life. Isn't that what you want?'

'Yes.' But she sounded doubtful.

'You did ask me to pray for you,' I reminded her. We were nearly at her house by now. 'I can pray for it to go and never come back, but only if that's what you want yourself.'

She hesitated again, then said, 'It is what I want. I am getting fed up with it. And frightened. Do you have to do anything special?'

A car had pulled up behind us and was flashing its headlights.

'That's a neighbour,' she said. 'You're in his parking place.'

I wound the window down and called out that we'd be gone in a second. There was nowhere else to park.

'There's no special formula,' I told Annette. 'We'll just say the "Our Father".'

So we sat in the car and said the prayer together, and when we got to the 'Deliver us from evil' I repeated it, and so did she. Then she got out of the car, and I drove home. Without getting lost or running out of petrol.

When I saw Annette again, she said, 'I phoned the bishop again and he said I didn't need deliverance; I'd dealt with it myself.'

Evil is the most boring thing on earth. It can only get itself the number of fans it has by masquerading as something exciting and attractive.

I have met even committed Christians who don't

believe in the reality of the devil. Yet Jesus Christ talked about him as a reality, and a dangerous nuisance to God's children. He referred to him on separate occasions as Lucifer, the prince of darkness, the prince of this world, and the father of lies, and Jesus was not into perpetuating fairy stories or humouring people's quaint old-fashioned ideas: he was into truth, no matter who found it unfashionable or offensive.

I believe the devil to be a personality wholly destroyed and consumed by evil, and committed to consuming and destroying other personalities. I have encountered several of his followers, and they have the bleakest and most negative spirits you could ever hope to avoid.

How anyone could turn the devil into a concept of daring, enlivening, sensational power, I don't know. Evil does have power – people give it power when they put their faith in it, because faith is a powerful gift from God. But any power that doesn't submit to God is solely destructive. It can't create, build up, or improve anyone's life.

But many people do believe in a world of supernatural energy that can be accessed and shared for human benefit, without any reference to Jesus Christ. Or else they use some form of 'Christ-concept' to justify supernatural exploration, replacing the real historical person of Jesus Christ who, as God's only son, told us clearly that he was the only route to the real supernatural power of goodness – God. The whole teaching of Jesus is based on the Old Testament – the commands of the one God, the God of Abraham, Isaac, and Jacob – which firmly forbade any dabbling in any form of occult activity.

When I first began praying with people, it was easy to

tell who was free in their spirit and who had allowed their power of choice to be overcome by some other entity. I just didn't find it easy to tell the difference between people who had got involved in occultism and people who were taking drugs. I always had to ask them which one they had done – because in spiritual terms the effects were very similar.

In both cases, the person had handed over control of their sanity and personality to some substance or entity that, by its very nature, was unpredictable. It would harm them in ways they might or might not recognize. They might simply become harder in their attitude, more resistant to God, and less open to sharing in the sufferings of their fellow human beings – in which case, they usually believed the drugs or the occult practices had had no effect on them at all, apart from making them feel more confident and less vulnerable.

Or they might have been affected in ways they could see and feel – which was more frightening for them, but probably safer, because then they knew they were not in control and needed help for their spirit and mind to be freed from an unwelcome influence.

Abby was the neighbour of a friend, who was concerned about her because she kept getting periods of depression, and anti-depressant tablets of various kinds had made no difference. She asked if she could bring Abby to see me one evening, so that we could both pray with her.

So Rachel and Abby came round, but when Abby started to tell me what had been troubling her, Rachel was startled to hear what she had to say.

'I didn't want to tell you, Rachel,' Abby explained, 'because I thought you might be frightened. So I said I just had depression. But what happened was that I felt somebody move into me – another person actually, physically, move into my body. And since then I've been hearing this person talking to me.'

'Saying what?' asked Rachel.

'The other day I heard, "My Jesus is stronger than your Jesus",' Abby told her. 'And when I asked, "Who is your Jesus, then?" it said, "Ronan".'

'Who's Ronan?' asked Rachel.

'He's a medium,' Abby said. 'I went along to a spiritualist meeting with a friend, because her mother had died and she wanted to contact her.'

'That's dangerous,' said Rachel.

'I know that now, but I didn't then,' Abby told her. 'This man Ronan picked me out and said he saw spirits standing around me, and that I was a natural psychic. He said I should go for training to become a medium. So I did. I went to a few sessions, and then I felt this – thing, person – move into me and I got really scared. And I keep getting these black waves of depression. Can you help me get rid of it?'

'Do you want to get rid of it?' I asked her, and Rachel said indignantly, 'Of course she does!'

But Abby said, 'I'm not saying I don't want to be a medium. I'm just saying there must be something wrong with this Ronan. He's doing it wrong. The other people were very nice.'

'So you don't want to let go of this spirit?'

'I do! I don't want to go on feeling like this. It feels as though my mind is not my own.'

'You'll have to let go of the whole thing,' I told her. 'All the involvement in spiritualism. You can't be a medium and have your mind free. Being a medium is about opening yourself to every spirit that comes along.'

'No, it isn't!' she protested. 'We were taught ways of protecting ourselves. If you do it right, you don't get harmed. And you don't harm anyone else,' she added fiercely.

'You've been harmed,' I pointed out.

'That's because of this person – this Ronan. He must be doing it for the wrong reasons.'

'They're all wrong reasons. God has forbidden mediumship. There are warnings all through the Bible – the Old Testament and the New Testament. If you want to help people who are grieving for someone they've lost, you direct them to God.'

'But you Catholics pray to saints!' she said. 'And they're all dead!'

'If people live for Christ and die in Christ, they aren't dead. They're living with him, in eternity. It makes no difference whether you chat to Rachel sitting next to you now on the sofa or whether you chat to someone who has lived for God and died at peace with him. You're still just chatting to a friend. You don't go to a spiritualist to do it through them.'

'But they can help! It's the same thing!'

There was an angry expression on Abby's face now, and Rachel was looking at her sideways. She had expected to be taking part in a simple prayer to relieve depression. This was a side of her friend she hadn't seen.

'No, they can't help. How could they help anyone, if they're doing something God has forbidden?'

'Why would he forbid it?' she challenged. 'Because it does help people, whatever you say.'

'He's forbidden it for very good reasons. You can end up in spiritual bondage – not free to think your own thoughts or make your own decisions. You can be manipulated, and not even know it.'

'Only if someone misuses their gift! Not if they use it properly!'

'The proper use of a gift is to subject it to God, and do what he says with it. If he says spiritualism is idolatry, we have to trust him.'

'But if you only accept the good spirits...?'

'We can't tell the difference. We think we can, but we can't. It's like a child being told there are nasty men out there so you mustn't get in a stranger's car. Then she gets in a stranger's car because he isn't nasty: he's very nice and smiling and buys her sweets.'

'I believe there are good spirits,' said Abby. 'Good people who have died and just want to talk to their loved ones here.'

'Sure. And if God allows them to talk to you, you will hear them. Through him. But some people die without knowing God, and they get a bit lost. The best you can do is to pray for them to find their way to God. There are also malicious spirits who will mimic someone you've loved and lost, and get you hooked on spiritism.'

She thought about it. Rachel was holding her hand and looking anxiously at her. Abby had to make a choice – to be a spiritist medium or to follow God. She couldn't do both.

'Has anyone ever made contact with you, after they died?' Abby asked me.

'Yes.'

'So – you just ignored them?'

'No. I prayed for them. One was my father-in-law, who died an atheist. I felt he was looking for help, so I told him his next step was to go to Jesus Christ now, not to me.'

'Did he contact you again after that?'

'No. He seemed relieved, and went.'

'Anyone else?'

'Plenty. Especially one friend, who died a difficult death but never stopped praying for people. We still pray for each other now.'

'You talk to her?'

'Yes, why not?'

'And she talks to you?'

'Well, I'd be very offended otherwise!'

'So you're a medium!' she said triumphantly.

'No. I talk to Jesus Christ. If he allows me to have a conversation with someone, I ask him to give me the words and give me the love – whether they're still living or they've died. Death isn't a big event. At times, I get told to be silent, or tell the person I'm not the right one to help them, or direct them to God, to pray for themselves. You conduct every relationship in the way that the Holy Spirit directs.'

'Has God ever told you not to talk to someone who has died?'

'Yes. I don't know why. Maybe my hearing might be distorted at that point, or maybe they'd dump on me a lot of distress that should be brought straight to God. But yes, there have been times when I've heard someone crying for help and God has told me to concentrate on him and leave whoever it is to him.'

'I still can't see the difference,' Abby said.

'I'm not sure I can explain it, because I'm sure I don't understand it all myself,' I said. 'But we don't have to understand everything. You just trust God and obey him. If he says no to something, he knows why. He says pray for the dead, talk to your friends who have died, don't forget them – but don't go looking for them, summoning up their spirits.'

'They might need to be left in peace,' Abby said.

'They might. Or there might be other reasons. Does it matter, if God says no?'

'And he's definitely said no to spiritualist meetings and seances and mediums?' she asked.

'Definitely. Categorically. Spelled out in no uncertain terms, throughout the Bible,' I confirmed.

'But I know Christians who go to seances! Ronan told me there are even vicars!'

'You can't be a practising Christian and be involved in spiritualism. Spiritualism is based on faith in death. To lose your fear of death, you go to Jesus Christ.'

She was silent for a long time, twisting her hands in her lap. Rachel sat beside her quietly. It wasn't going to be an easy decision for Abby.

Finally she said, 'OK. I don't want anything to do with this spirit stuff. How do I get out of it?'

'You've done it, the moment you decide you don't want it,' I told her. 'Now we just pray, and you tell Jesus Christ you'll give him a free hand in your life. You'll take what he gives, and let him take away anything that doesn't lead you closer to him.'

'OK.' She bowed her head and we prayed. Afterwards, she smiled but said, 'Is that it? What if it comes back?'

'You seem OK to me,' I said, 'but if you're worried I can arrange for you to see a priest. You can have a more formal form of deliverance.'

'What would that involve?'

'More prayer. A blessing. An anointing.'

'Would it be painful?'

'Are you thinking of *The Exorcist*?'

She laughed. 'Yes!'

'It won't be like that. Let me know if you want me to arrange it. See how you are in the week.'

She phoned during the week and said she felt fine, but still felt nervous that it might come back. So I rang a priest who was reassuringly normal and down-to-earth and asked if Abby could have some prayer for deliverance, and he made an appointment.

'Though if it's complicated,' he said, 'we might need to call in the diocesan exorcist.'

'It doesn't seem that bad,' I said, 'but see what you think when you see her.'

Rachel again came with Abby, and the three of us went into the sacristy to wait for the priest.

Abby was interested in her surroundings. 'I've never been in a Catholic church,' she said. 'What's this room for?'

'It's where the priest prepares to say Mass, and where the vestments and chalices are kept.'

She pointed to a Latin inscription above the crucifix. 'What does that say?'

'Jesus Christ, risen from death, alive for ever.'

She looked startled. 'You believe that?'

'Oh yes.'

She stared at me. 'It's real, then? I mean, you believe he's really alive? Now?'

'Now. Here. Yes. He promised to be with us until the end of time. Then we'd be with him. Beyond time.'

'Wow,' she said softly.

The priest came in and had a chat with Abby about what had happened to her. She was nervous, and at the end of it he said, 'I can pray over you, but you don't need it. You've dealt with this yourself, by your own common sense in rejecting it. So I'm just going to bless you with holy water and say a quick prayer for your protection in future.'

He blessed Rachel as well, and me, and we were outside the church in a very short time. Abby was relieved.

'That was nothing like *The Exorcist*!' she said, with a huge sigh. 'I'm going to go home now and sleep for a week!'

17

Abby's involvement with the occult had been accidental. More serious problems occur when people deliberately seek out experiences of the paranormal and supernatural, perhaps with the hope of attaining more power over their future, or control of other people. Although they may intend originally to use that power for good – their own or others' – in fact, as Jesus said, only God is good.

A few years ago, I went with a priest to a parish a long distance from home, to do a healing service.

It was several hours' drive, and we prayed on the way. We were fasting, which is often a good preparation for healing prayer. However, physical stamina has never been a great gift of mine, and sometimes I have to eat if I get too weak or light-headed.

It's not that fasting is a good thing in itself: it's a tool, to be used when appropriate. It can be a form of prayer and can also help you to keep a clear mind, not distracted by a lot of digestive activity going on at the same time! But if hunger itself becomes a distraction, it's better to eat.

But on this occasion I was fine.

We arrived at the presbytery – the house attached to the church, where the priests lived – and were welcomed by the priest who had asked for the healing service to be held. There were two older priests there as well, who were non-committal about healing, but quite friendly.

Father Seamus showed us into a room where we could prepare for the service, and said, 'When you're ready, come downstairs. We've a grand dinner prepared.'

Father Adam stopped him. 'We fast before healing services,' he said.

'Well, you won't be fasting today,' Seamus said firmly. 'I asked the housekeeper to come in specially, though it's her day off, and there's a big roast which we're not going to eat on our own! Five minutes, all right?'

Adam wasn't happy, but I felt this was all right: even, that it had come from God. Although I'd felt fine on the drive there, ever since we'd come into the house, I felt weird. I hoped the food would help.

The meal was nice, though a bit strained as the older priests asked Adam a lot of questions about why he felt the need for healing. Wasn't the Mass enough, they said?

Adam was used to this. As a priest involved in healing, he was often regarded as an oddity by members of the priesthood who were not. So he answered quite happily that sometimes people needed the personal touch of God – to know that he was interested in their individual lives and wanted to help. It fostered faith, he said.

'What about raising false hopes?' asked one of the priests. 'If people think they'll be healed of their illnesses and they aren't, they'll be disappointed.'

Father Adam helped himself to a roast potato.

'This is very good,' he told Seamus. 'You're treating us royally. Thank you.'

He turned to the other priest and said, 'False hope in God? If that's who they place their hope in, it won't be false. They may not get what they want, in every case, but they won't be disappointed. They'll only be disappointed in us, their priests, if we don't take the trouble to pray with them for their needs.'

'But why the necessity for laying on hands? Why not just say a prayer for them, like we always have done?' the other priest said.

'We're physical beings as well as spiritual,' Adam explained.

Father Seamus suddenly said, 'We have some strange goings on in this parish. None of them good. There are fourteen Satanist covens in this area, and they fast and pray and offer sacrifice for the failure of every project we have.'

Adam put down his fork. 'Is that why you've asked us to come here?'

'Partly. Last year we set up a charitable project, for helping the poor. We had a fine man in charge of it, very committed. A strong young chap, in the best of health. This Satanist woman had been converted and was coming here to our church, and she told us that her group had a project to destroy this man, and that within a year he would be dead.

'We took no notice at all. But within the year, he was dead. A sudden heart attack. So we've begun to take it more seriously now. They mean business. The lady told us they are focusing most of their attention on the Catholic churches, because we believe in the sacraments. We believe the Eucharist is the real physical presence of Christ and it has real power. And they find that a threat.'

Adam pushed his plate away. 'Terrific meal,' he said. 'Let's go and thank your housekeeper. Then we must pray.'

We headed for the upstairs room, but I needed to go to the loo first. While I was in there, I was overcome with dizziness and felt as though I would faint.

'Lord, you brought us here,' I prayed. 'And I want to help. So, unless I'm more use to you sick, would you please deal with this?'

Heaviness and tiredness swamped me, so much that all I wanted to do was lie down on the small square of none-too-clean carpet in the toilet and go to sleep for hours.

'Father, if this is oppression from some spirit wanting to interfere with the healing service, please lift it,' I prayed.

It lifted.

I went out and found Adam asleep in a chair.

'Shall we pray now?' I said loudly.

He opened one eye and said, 'Give me ten minutes. I feel sleepy after that meal.'

'It could be oppression,' I said. 'Fourteen covens in one area?'

'Oh, yes,' he said sleepily. 'Could be.'

'We need to pray,' I said.

'Fine. There's a prayer in my breviary for deliverance and protection from evil. We'll use that.' His eyes were still closed.

'Adam. Where's your breviary?'

'In the car. You go and get it and I'll just have a few minutes'....' He was too drowsy to finish the sentence.

'I'm going to start praying now,' I said, 'while you go down to the car and fetch the book.' I started praying aloud. Very aloud. Sleep through that!

He opened his eyes, shocked at my rudeness in telling him to fetch his own book. But it worked. He went down to the car, returned with the breviary, and prayed with authority, commanding any spirit not subject to the name of Jesus to depart.

In the first five minutes of the service, a woman was healed. It was lovely to see. She was a mother in her thirties, with her husband and two children with her, and she had been permanently confined to a wheelchair for eleven years, following an operation that had gone wrong and damaged her hip joints.

She was determined to receive whatever God chose to give her – whether healing, or patience to cope with her disability and strength to give her children all they needed from her. Her eleven-year-old son was in front of me as she was prayed with. He was praying for his mother with his whole being. Every part of his body and soul was engaged in the prayer for her to be well. I had never seen a child pray so fervently.

When she got up and walked the length of the aisle and back, he was frozen to the spot at first, then turned to his father and cried. His father called him to help him fold the wheelchair up and put it in the car. 'We won't be needing this again,' he told him.

After this healing, the other people in the church really opened up and expected God to work for them as well. And he did.

Adam was concerned that the woman who had walked would need follow-up prayer, especially in a parish surrounded by such malice. It turned out that the family came from a different area and had heard about the service from a friend, so Adam was able to put them in touch with a prayer group in their own locality.

It's easy for someone who is healed at a service, supported by everyone's prayer, to lose faith afterwards when they're alone or subjected to other people's doubts. I'd noticed that, in the gospel accounts of healings by Jesus, he often told people not to tell anyone about their healing, or to go straight home or to the priest and not to stay around people who wanted to discuss the event. Faith needs protection, and a recently healed person can be a target for people who don't want to believe and are hoping the person's health will fail.

It would be wrong to doubt the power of evil, or to dismiss the threats of its followers as rubbish. We have power from God to do good, and it is real power. But we all have a choice, and if some people choose to divert that power and use it for destructive purposes, the effect on the lives of other people can be – literally – diabolical.

But there is no power stronger than God, and he is very willing to use his power, as long as we're not misled into thinking we can cope with evil very well by ourselves and don't need help.

I used to think evil and good were obvious opposites, like night and day. You didn't need to be a genius to tell the difference. Then the Lord told me that evil mimics good. Half the people it attracts don't want to be bad. It's goodness they're looking for. But they forget that only God is good, and only he knows what real goodness is.

What's wrong with God? Why does he allow such suffering in the world? If he's so powerful and knowledgeable, how come he doesn't seem to know how to make us happy?

But his instructions for being happy have to be followed, by choice. If the owner of a valuable and sensitive piece of equipment doesn't follow the manufacturer's instructions, they needn't be surprised if the product blows up in their face.

If anyone wonders, though, why the people who do evil survive and it's the innocent and vulnerable who suffer, they may not yet have discussed with God how he sees people. The ones they are seeing as powerful evil tyrants may be spiritual weaklings – ignorant and poverty-stricken souls. And the ones they see as useless to society, or as helpless victims – old people, sick people, disabled or mentally handicapped adults and children, unborn embryos – are strong souls, regularly crucified and repeatedly rising above it.

If we only knew how much we owe the 'useless' people, and how much our society needs them, we would regard them as celebrities, and give them more help in dealing with their enemies – frustration, lack of confidence, and temptations to bitterness. As it is, they may have to wait till after their death before anyone recognizes their impressive contribution to society.

If occult activity or interest can provide a loophole for evil to enter someone's life, another entry point can be personal sin.

Sin is an outmoded concept for some. Even those who do accept that they're capable of it, and that it's destructive, tend to think they can deal with it. A simple acknowledgment to God that they have done wrong will result in forgiveness and the removal of the blot on their personality.

It's not always quite so simple. The early disciples of Jesus advised people, 'Confess your sins *to one another*.'

One reason could be that sin is a wound, and a wound needs healing. It's not always best to bandage up your own injuries; they may not be easily accessible or you may be too weak to do it.

An apparently straightforward sin – like telling a lie, for example – can cover up a more difficult problem. A good spiritual confidant, praying to God for guidance, can help pinpoint the underlying cause of a repeated sin, and will pray for you to be strengthened in that particular area of your life.

A formal confession and prayer of repentance is in itself humbling, and can help the soul open up to more help from God. And being forgiven by another person, acting under the authority of Jesus, who told everyone, 'Forgive one another', is a real asset in the surprisingly difficult task of forgiving yourself.

Sometimes, a person's life has acquired an evil element that trips them up when they're sincerely determined to do good, simply because they've forgotten about a sin. They've buried it, rather than bringing it out to the light to be dealt with, forgiven, and have any damage to their character made good.

Jack was in this situation. He was a most unlikely candidate for evil – a large, slow, quiet man who suffered from crippling shyness. I met him on a retreat and invited him to come and pray sometime, because he said he greatly needed confidence. His lack of it was preventing him from going any further with his career.

He called round, apologizing for being two minutes late, for having muddy shoes, for banging his head on the door frame as he entered the room, for making a scraping noise with the chair before he sat down, and almost for existing.

As he was so embarrassed, I made no attempt at small talk and suggested we got down to prayer immediately. I explained that I often laid hands on people to pray, but said if that would make him uncomfortable I needn't do it. He said he would like 'every gift in the book that God would like to give me,' so I made the sign of the cross and prepared to pray.

'Stand behind him,' I suddenly heard from the Holy Spirit. 'Don't stand in front of him; his spirit is violent and you'll be thrown against the wall. Also, don't touch him as lightly as you normally do. He needs a sign that the Father can deal with him with a firm hand.'

So I stood behind him and laid hands on him firmly, though it seemed an extreme thing to do. The poor man was so inoffensive I couldn't believe he would swat a fly without apologizing, let alone throw me against a wall!

Yet as I prayed, something seemed to arise from him – a smouldering fury, followed by a huge escape of force – like steam shooting out of the funnel of a pressure cooker.

Jack heaved a great sigh as I finished praying and said, 'That feels better.'

'Is there anything you want to talk about?' I asked him. 'Shall I make us a cup of tea?'

He looked alarmed and said, 'No,' and left straight away. But a while later he phoned and said he would like to come again, and he had something to tell me.

He had been involved in a murder, he said, when he was settled at the table with a cup of tea in his hand. He hadn't been the one to carry it out, but he had known about it and hadn't done anything to stop it, because he was curious. Also, he had made half-joking attempts to threaten the life of a member of his family and when this didn't attract much notice, the attempts had become more serious, and could have succeeded on one occasion.

I encouraged him to go to the priest and ask for

confession, and he said he would, but it was some time before he got up the courage to approach the only priest he knew and ask to see him.

In the meantime, I found I was feeling weighed down by the admission of guilt he had made but hadn't allowed to be dealt with. The Lord had said it was important he went for formal confession, so I had made it clear to him that my forgiveness wasn't sufficient; he must go himself and make his peace with the Lord. The fact that Jack found it so hard to do this may have been an indication that it was really important.

So I did something I hadn't thought I would do. I went to see the priest myself, and told him that somebody's sin was weighing on me. I felt somehow involved in the guilt, by knowing about it, but I wasn't in a position to offer absolution. I could hardly confess a sin that was somebody else's, and I was afraid it might be gossip to tell the priest what another person had done. So before I told him anything, I asked him about the situation, in theory.

The priest thought about it and said he could see it would be quite a burden to know such a thing about somebody and he would pray for that to be lifted. As for gossip or breaking confidences, he said he was often told things in confidence and found it an advantage: he could pray for the person and was ready when they came to talk to him themselves. In some way, he felt the ground had been prepared and they found it easier to broach a difficult subject, because they sensed that he was expecting to hear it and wouldn't reject them.

Confiding information about a person was *not* gossip, he said, only if you loved and cared for the person and wanted them to be understood, not judged, and if you believed that the person you were telling would care for them, not judge them and not repeat the information to anybody.

That sounded safe enough, so I told him, and the following week Jack told me he had summoned up the courage to go and receive the sacrament of reconciliation (confession) and had felt much lighter since.

It sometimes seems that Christians pay inordinate attention to sin and guilt. Many people believe it's healthier, when you've done something wrong, to forget it and move on. But forgetting isn't the same as receiving forgiveness from God, and long-forgotten sin can have long-term effects.

The only purpose of all this pernickety practice of identifying and confessing sin is freedom – to be free of all hidden inhibitions that prevent us from being the person we really want to be.

I met a crowd of old friends after many years' absence and was surprised to find that the ones who had been the 'wild child' of their particular circle were rather conventional and undemonstrative now. The ones who had been good and quiet and were sometimes regarded as cold or not very fun-loving, on the other hand, were warm and affectionate and uninhibited.

Breaking all the rules can feel like fun and freedom at the time. But someone who has a string of 'close encounter' relationships, not based on God's idea of intimacy which takes time and self-restraint, can end up carrying all those people in spirit and it can make them feel very weighed down.

God is not going to be heavy on someone who did what seemed fine at the time. With him, it doesn't matter what state you arrive in, or at how late or early a stage in your life you come to him. You'll always get an exuberant welcome – and an offer to take off your shoulders the great heavy backpack of experiences that have turned out to be more than you need now, and far too heavy to go on carrying.

I used to think repentance was about remorse: that I had to be totally abjectly regretful about a lot of the things I had done, deny the validity of even the learning experience, and start afresh with the intention of making no more mistakes ever again.

It took me a long while to understand that God doesn't reject anything – even the things you wish you hadn't done. He won't obliterate your life history, because even though it got covered in mud there are glimpses of gold in it. He will wash the mud away so you can enjoy the gold bits.

I was always told God was good. But nobody ever told me how nice he was.

18

CHAPTER

Many years ago, I was on holiday on a beautiful sunny island, and a friend introduced me to snorkelling. I had thought this was something annoying that little boys did in swimming pools, and couldn't see the point of it as a no-longer-young woman. The rubber mask also reminded me of being given general anaesthetic at the dentist's as a child, so I wasn't at all keen to try wearing it.

But once I'd seen my first fish, I was a snorkelling convert. Wearing flippers, too, was terrific for a poor swimmer – like wearing seven-league boots in the sea; one flip of the toes carried you forward for *miles*!

When I ventured out on my own round a small jutting outcrop of rock, I felt very daring. Visions of man-eating sharks and over-affectionate octopi were firmly banished from my imagination, but the first jolt of fear came when the smooth sandy seabed a few metres beneath me suddenly fell away dramatically in a sheer rocky drop to a far deeper stretch of ocean.

Immediately, I heard the Lord say, 'You can't fall; you're in the wrong element,' and I realized that's what my fear was – of falling. I wasn't used to seeing underwater, and reacted as I would have done if I'd been walking and suddenly found myself on the edge of a sheer cliff drop.

In fact, it was easier in the deep water: there was more weight of water to hold the swimmer up and less effort required to lie flat on the surface of it and be carried along by the mere idle flip of a toe.

'When you live in my Spirit too, you're in the wrong element to fall,' the Lord continued.

This was great! Not only to learn to snorkel, to meet fish in their own territory and to overcome my fear of heights, but spiritual direction under water as well!

'Swim closer to the rock,' the Lord said now. 'I want to show you more of my creation.'

I was amazed how close the fish came – almost nose to nose; their curiosity at meeting me seemed equal to my delight in seeing them.

A big shoal of fish swam by and it occurred to me to follow them, as they were the experts under water – they must know where they were going!

But that familiar voice came again: 'Don't follow them; they're only creatures, not the creator. They follow the prevailing spirit, whatever it is at the time; you must only follow my Spirit.'

One of my friends caught up with me and gestured to me to keep going, round the headland to the next bay. I was a bit uncertain, but willing to try, so I followed.

The next bay was even more beautiful than the first one, and deserted because there was no beach, just the rock face dropping down into the water. In the centre of it was a hollow. It looked like a cave, but it was impossible to tell how far back it went. It was dark inside.

My friend gestured to go towards the cave, but I shook my head. There was a strong current of dark water flowing into it and I wasn't a strong swimmer. I didn't think it would be a good idea to get into the flow of the current and be swept towards the cave.

'Just to have a look,' John encouraged, removing his snorkel to talk. 'We needn't go in.'

I didn't want to talk in case my mask fogged up, as I wasn't too competent at clearing it and putting it back on on in deep water, so I just shook my head again. He swam round me and took my arm and swam forwards – into the current. I signalled no with my hand and turned back, but he circled me again.

'It would be interesting to see how deep the cave is,' he said. 'We can always come out again.'

Again, I shook my head. No. We had been on a trip to the centre of the island where we had seen an inland lake and been told that the island had an unusual phenomenon – at some point, the tide of the sea flowed into an underground river and surfaced here in this lake, instead of the usual situation of a river rising at some inland spring and flowing out to sea.

For all we knew, this dark sweep of current flowing towards the rock might be the starting point of the incoming underground stream. I had no ambition to be sucked underground and surface in some mangled form – if at all – in the centre of the island!

But wherever I swam John was nudging me towards the current while he – a stronger swimmer anyway – stayed outside the range of it.

Eventually, panicked, and with the Lord's warning about never following the prevailing spirit still fresh with me, I pulled out the snorkel mouthpiece, shouted, 'No, I don't want to go into the cave,' and swam away from him.

He followed me, caught hold of me, and said, 'Don't worry! Look, we'll be fine!'

I was right on the edge of the current now; I could

feel the tug of it, and he was preventing me from swimming forwards out of it. 'Get out of my way,' I said. 'I'm getting pulled in.'

He laughed and stayed treading water.

I gave a huge kick with my flipper, clear of the current, pushed him roughly aside, yelled, 'Get out of my fucking way!' and shot past him and away from him, and didn't stop swimming until I reached the beach.

At the end of the holiday, he was still commenting on my 'rude behaviour' and the way I had spoken to him. He was very hurt, he said, that I would speak in such a rude way to a friend.

I wonder if sometimes we see God as treating us the same way. We can't always see where he's leading, and sometimes he seems to be shoving us rather than leading. He lets us get into situations we feel totally inadequate to deal with, and seems to take no notice when we tell him we're frightened.

Then, if we express how we really feel about the way he's treating us, we're afraid we'll be condemned. How could we be so ungrateful to the good and loving God who is our friend? Is he ever going to forgive us, if we stop being polite and pretending to be quite happy with the way he lets us drift into dark waters and feel our security sucked away by currents too strong to swim against?

So we try to pretend we trust him, when really we've known since childhood that it's madness to trust anyone who doesn't take any notice when we say no. And we keep on repeating the same polite-request prayers, when if we were really honest we'd shout at him and tell him to stop messing about with our safety and risking our lives.

But God is not just with us, swimming alongside. He

is always exactly where we are – not an arm's length away, in a place where he can ensure his own safety. And he never asked us to be polite. Jesus always had more time for people who were blunt and honest than for people who said the right things but didn't mean them.

The Psalms, and the books of the prophets, in the Old Testament, are full of potentially holy, terrified people crying out to God. Not 'crying out' as in loud exultant prayers, but crying, sobbing, screaming, shouting – yes, and effing and blinding and calling him all the names under heaven. Accusing him of letting them drown while others float calmly to safety.

We live in dangerous times. There are occasions when it's only reasonable to be afraid. And times when it isn't a problem to feel you can trust nobody. People are only creatures, not the creator. If they're not listening to you, they're not listening to God, and at those times it's no good following them. They're only following the prevailing spirit. And that spirit may be curiosity; the kind of curiosity that didn't do Adam and Eve much good. There are times when it's not good to know all there is to know, or to try all the things you haven't tried yet.

God doesn't take risks with us. It may feel like a great risk, to do what he says, at times. He can lead you to the edge of your security and beyond it. But it's only a risk when you don't follow his prompting but rely on human effort or human help instead, or 'play it safe' by going along with what the majority, or the strongest character, seems to want.

The great news is, if you follow God's directions, you can't possibly fail. Even if you fall over the edge of the cliff – lose your footing in life and lose all your security – you can't possibly come to harm. You are in the wrong element to fall and will only find yourself held up by the sheer, clear depth of his Spirit.

It's right to fear evil. It's only natural to fear the unknown. But as soon as you feel you're out of your depth and have reached your own limits, don't be polite with God. Yell. Tell him what you think of him, in the most outspoken terms.

Just don't drift along, pretending you trust him when you don't. If you drift, you may find you've stopped listening to his Spirit and are just going with the flow: the human one that doesn't know where it's going.

19

If God could do miracles, and apparently wanted to do them, I wondered why there were not more of them around.

My definition of a miracle, though, was an instant, total, recognizable change that couldn't be explained in any other way except by the direct intervention of God. Miracles of that kind would turn people's lives upside down. I didn't know too many people who would want their lives turned upside down.

Love, on the other hand, set people back on their feet. It was a gentle, persevering process of help, understanding, and forgiveness. I didn't know anyone that didn't suit. A lot of people were afraid of love, in theory, but in practice, love – without strings attached – turned out to be exactly what they wanted. And the effect on their lives was miraculous.

Father Nathan was one of the most loving people I'd met. When he started work in a neighbouring parish, all kinds of people who would rather have lain down in front of a ten-ton truck than go near a church began to gravitate towards it.

How he persuaded some of them not only to come to church but to join a charismatic prayer group was a mystery known only to Nathan and God himself. But the account of one of those people, Tess, is an example of both the step-by-step patient process of God's love and the more dramatic, instant miracle.

Even when an 'instant success' occurs, it is never as instant as it appears. It has been preceded by years of God's patient, persistent love for that person, and it will be followed by the same processes of suffering, doubt, and fear as those experienced by Christians who have never known a miracle in their lives.

Tess had been a prostitute for twenty years when she first met Father Nathan. She had been to convent school as a child, and it occurred to her that although she had fallen from grace with God, it was a pity for her children to have to miss out. It wasn't their fault, she reasoned, that they had her for a mother, and they deserved the chance to have their own contact with God. Other children in their school were talking about making their First Communion, and parents were invited to go to their local priest to make the arrangements.

Tess lived near the church, but she never went near it. She had often seen Father Nathan getting in or out of his car outside, and thought he looked human and not too frightening. So one day, as he drove up and parked, she buttonholed him and asked about sending her children to Communion classes. He invited her to call in at the parish office and have their names put on the list.

She did that, then had doubts. What if someone told the priests what she was? She wouldn't want her children to suffer any critical glances or comments, or be treated any differently from the rest. She decided that if there was a chance that the priest might send the children away, she had better find out in advance.

So she accosted Nathan again, as he arrived in his car to say Mass.

'Before you take my children for First Communion, there are some things I ought to tell you about myself,' she said, in a rush. 'I'm a prostitute and I have been for twenty years, and I don't mean years ago, either – I mean last night, I was going round the pubs, here, in this area. My working name's Yasmin. So if people tell you things about me, they're probably true, but I want my children to come into the church and make their First Communion with the rest.'

'Get in the car,' he said.

She hesitated. 'It might not look good, for you.'

'Don't worry what it looks like.'

She got into the car and talked to him, and he prayed with her there and then.

The following week, he brought her to the prayer meeting, arriving late – she had nearly lost her nerve.

The room was full that week – Nathan had been doing his work – and there were several faces I didn't know. His gift was to bring in everybody in need, and the needs of the people there were so acute that nothing would have helped them except God.

There were people who were seriously ill, people in the throes of bereavement or divorce, addicts, alcoholics, people with mental illness, sexual disorders, disfigurements, and emotional problems. There were people who had been abandoned, abused, or neglected as children. There were women, and men, who had been raped. There were homosexuals who were not glad to be gay and couldn't come to terms with it; people who were suicidal because they couldn't live with who they were or what they had done or what had been done to them;

people who were terminally lonely and unable to make contact with the people who lived all around them. And there was Tess.

She had the most frightened face I had ever seen. Everything about her spelt out extreme fear. My first thought on seeing her was, 'What is wrong with her? God, help her!'

As the meeting got under way, her eyes kept flicking round the faces of the people there. I tried to catch her eye and smile, but she never settled on one person's face long enough to see them. She kept making lightning circuits with her eyes, which always returned to one place – the door. At any minute, I expected her to leap out of her seat and make a run for it. But she managed to stay there.

Afterwards, when I knew her, she told me that she had felt like the devil – the one black soul in a room full of holy people all peaceful and serene, singing hymns. Appearances can certainly be deceptive!

The crunch came when it was time to start the healing prayer. That week, it was Nathan and Carrie who went round the group from one person to another, laying hands on each one while the whole group prayed for them.

Tess's anxiety seemed to increase. She sat forward on her chair, gripping the edge of it, watching with sheer terror as Nathan and Carrie moved gradually towards her. When they were two or three people away from her, I began to pray in earnest that she wouldn't run away and that God would give her whatever she needed. I couldn't see how anyone could be so afraid and go on living a normal everyday life. Surely if she didn't get help, here and now, she wouldn't survive?

She sat poised for flight, her eyes never leaving the door now. Nathan and Carrie were with the person next to her. Then with Tess.

She shrank back, staring up at their faces as they stood by her. Then, as they laid hands on her, an expression of wonderment came over her face. She raised her hands in the air and fell to her knees, looking upwards with rapt attention, completely still, apart from her lips moving slightly.

Nathan prayed with her a little while longer, then they both moved on. Tess stayed where she was, transfixed. Transformed.

I went to talk to her afterwards. 'Do you mind me asking what happened to you tonight?'

'I was in heaven,' she said simply. 'One moment the only thing I could think of was, "I have to get out of here," and the next – I was just in heaven. I feel happier than I've ever felt in my life. I know Jesus is with me – here.'

'Tomorrow you may find you come down to earth with a crash,' I warned her, 'but he will still be with you. Whether you feel it or not.'

Nathan warned of the same thing. He told her Jesus would help her if she felt tempted to become depressed. It was common to have a reaction after such an experience.

But Tess stayed elated and happy for months. She sang all day long and studied the Bible avidly. When anyone called round to see her, she instantly invited them to pray, and never seemed to grow tired: she could pray for hours. A line in a hymn that meant something to her, or a paragraph in the Bible that told her something she hadn't known about God, were enough to make her happy all day.

She ran down to see Nathan early one morning, soon after her experience in the prayer meeting, and said the Lord had told her to start healing people. He was understandably cautious. These gifts are given by the Lord, he said, but they take time to develop. There's a period of training, and during that time the soul that has newly found God needs solitude and prayer, and study of the Bible, and good counsel. Nothing should be hurried. If she was to start healing people, time would make it clear.

'That's what I thought myself,' she said. 'And anyway, I haven't a clue how it's done. But I was woken up in the middle of the night, and the Lord showed me how to lay hands on people, and said I was to do it like this.' She demonstrated.

This gave Nathan a shock, because it was exactly the way I had been taught by the Lord to lay on hands as well. I had never been shown by anyone else, and the method looked rather eccentric, but he had seen it work well for me! He asked Tess if she had been talking to me or had seen me pray with someone and she said no. He knew I had not been the one who had prayed with her that evening. He asked me to pray about her, and he would pray as well. We would ask for God's will for Tess to be made known.

The conventional way, for someone so recently converted, would be to keep a low profile and learn from the longer-established Christians in the community. But Tess was bursting with the love of God. It seemed that maybe that's what she had been trying to do all along – love people. She just hadn't chosen the right way. Was it God's will for her to wait, and be patient and humble – or for her to share the fruits of her faith and joy with other people, who could certainly benefit from it?

The answer was unequivocal. Tess had done her training. She had had an appalling childhood, and her adult life had been deprived of joy and comfort. Yet she had kept caring about people, and her younger brothers and sisters were full of stories about her kindness to them, even when she was going through her own most troubled times.

The best – and the only – training for healing was suffering. There are no healers in God's employ except wounded ones. Tess's wounds were obvious, but they were no worse than anyone else's, and less severe than some. We're all sinners, after all, and only God is good. She could pray with whoever she wanted, subject to the priest's authority.

She was a terrific asset to the group. People found her easy to confide in. She was open about her own shortcomings and failures, and completely unshockable by anyone else's confessions. She had time for everyone and never thought of confining her ministry to the church. If she met someone on the bus or in the supermarket who looked troubled and admitted they needed help, she would pray with them there and then if they wanted.

There were dark times ahead for Tess. There can be more venom in the hearts of respectable people than in any outright sinners. For a while Tess was protected, by her own happiness and by her friends. Much of the malice that would have been turned on her got diverted towards Nathan and towards me, for being instrumental in allowing a prostitute – or a very recent ex-prostitute – to pray over people.

She hadn't done courses in healing, the critics pointed out – and neither had Nathan, and neither had I.

She didn't use the right language to refer to spiritual things. She hadn't served her time. She was too happy. It was a sign of naivety. We were all behaving like children, thinking God was about fun and games.

But Tess had served her apprenticeship. She knew how to love, and she carried on loving, year in and year out. She had some terribly dark times, when her past caught up with her and seemed to strangle all the joy out of her present life. But each time, she responded to prayer and picked herself up and carried on.

She's a grandmother now. And a very good friend of mine. And a miracle – but then, she was always that.

20

CHAPTER

If a person's spirit doesn't die, then it certainly doesn't sleep. It's always worth praying with someone in a deep coma, or apparently lifeless. I have had the experience of being in a coma myself, and know that even when it's impossible to respond, to hear or to think, something can be transmitted to the spirit. I definitely felt the difference when people were in the room praying. It was much stronger than if they were just sitting there worrying or thinking.

So it didn't seem a waste of time, when a Filipino family asked a local lay minister who did healing services to go and pray with their sister in the Intensive Care Unit of one of the city hospitals. I went with him, and we prayed with the family in the waiting room before going in to see her. They were very upset.

When we saw her, she was deeply unconscious. The nurses said there had been no response from her since she had been admitted, over a week ago now. There was no movement or sign of life. She was connected to some sophisticated apparatus and had a tube in her throat and gel pads on her eyes to stop them drying out.

It took quite a while to get through to her spirit. When I did, all I heard was, 'I can't go on. I'm so tired.'

We both stopped praying at the same time, and

compared notes. He had heard the same thing – 'Too tired to live.' It seemed kinder to leave her as she was. But would the family be able to accept it?

Her collapse had been sudden, with no apparent warning. I asked her sister whether she had been very tired before she fell ill.

She had six children to support, her sister told us, back in the Philippines. Her husband couldn't find work and she was here to try to make money for them all. She worked long hours in a physically demanding job, and sent home every penny she could.

It sounded like sheer drudgery. And it seemed as though God had taken pity on her, and let her off the hook.

But her brothers and sisters wanted to know what would happen to the family. She was the strong one. The husband and the children relied on her for financial support. And they themselves relied on her as well: she was always so positive and cheerful.

They wanted us to keep praying; to go back into the unit and pray with her some more. But it just didn't seem kind. She had been everybody's life support, and now she was only surviving by means of a life-support system of her own. We could only pray that soon she would receive real support, in the arms of God, and that he would provide her family with other means of supporting one another.

It is terribly hard for families to see that death may be a gift God is giving to one of their members, not a disaster he is bringing on them. Many ask for prayer to save or revive their relative, at any cost, and may not be ready to consider how much it may cost that person to go on living.

Some people have simply fulfilled their mission in this life and are ready to move on. If begged hard enough to stay, they may summon up the effort and the will to ask God to give them more time, for the sake of their loved ones who would find it too hard to do without them.

But there comes a time when they simply can't find it in themselves to hang on any longer. Then it makes it easier for them if somebody loves them enough to pray for exactly what they want for themselves, whether it's to have the strength to stay and finish something they want to do, or whether it's to go.

Sally was a young woman who had developed cancer, had it treated apparently successfully, then found it recurred, and progressed very fast. It was soon pronounced untreatable and, because she said firmly she didn't want any kindly lies, the doctor told her she had only a few months to live.

I saw her at home before she went into the hospice, and then in the hospice, and each time she said the same thing: she didn't want to upset anybody. She felt guilty about dying.

'It's not your fault,' I told her, and she sighed and said she knew that, but she still felt it.

The last time I saw her, she was in a lot of pain and the morphine was making her feel groggy.

'What do you want me to pray for?' I asked her. 'To stay or to go?'

'If I'm not going to get better, I'd rather go soon,' she said. 'Is that selfish of me?'

'No.'

But something about the phrase 'if I'm not going to get better' bothered me.

'Do you feel content with your life?' I asked her. 'That

you've lived a good life? Been a good person?'

'No,' she said. 'There are lots of things I've done wrong. I keep trying, but...'

'But you never get any better?'

She was silent, then said, 'I've always tried to be there for my family. As far back as I remember, my mum and dad were always arguing and fighting. I tried to get between them, to make them calm down and listen to one another. And I tried to protect my younger brother and sister from getting too affected by the rows, so at least they had some home life.'

'But now you've had enough?'

'I haven't been as patient as I'd like. To be honest, I feel fed up with them. They're still fighting. Even here, when they come to see me. They'll never grow up.'

'Never get any better.'

'No. I've felt like a tree in the middle of the family, and they're all hanging on to me.'

'God doesn't ask you to do that,' I told her. 'He wants you to let go of them so they hang on to him. Even if they fall first.'

'They will!'

'Only into his hands. Their problems aren't terminal; they're just not accepting the remedy.'

'My problem is terminal,' she said.

'Do you want it to be?'

She went quiet for a minute, then said, 'I've had enough pain. I can't take any more.'

'OK.'

'You can't pray for that, can you?'

'For God to take you home? Sure.'

'I thought you could only pray for healing,' she said.

'It is healing. If it's what you want. And if it's right for you, it'll work for your family as well.'

'It isn't selfish, to ask to die? Are you sure?'

'I'm sure. You've done your part. And more. Shall we pray now?'

'Yes,' she said. 'You pray for me. And if I can do anything for you...'

'Get the champagne out for me when I arrive,' I said. 'I want a big welcome when I come to join you.'

She laughed. 'You'll get one; don't worry. It's been nice to know you.'

'And you. And I'll see you again.'

I laid hands on her and prayed, and afterwards she sat very still and didn't look up even when I went out and closed the door.

Her mother said she spent the next two days having conversations with relatives who were not there physically, talking to them about things she felt were unfinished, apologizing to people she felt she had hurt. Some were living and some had died. Then she pointed upwards and ahead of her and said, 'I have to go up those few steps and through that white door,' and shortly afterwards she died. Her family had come to terms with the fact that she was going to die, and they did let her go.

But for another person, Irma, it was a real wrench to accept that her brother was not going to live, and that finding someone to rescue him from death might not be in his interests.

Irma arrived at my house with her husband, very wound up, pouring out words very fast. It seemed best to let her talk herself out before we attempted to pray, but it took three and a half hours. For three of those, she talked without a break.

She had always been close to her brother. They had

grown up in Pakistan and the whole family was close, but she and her brother especially. As they grew older, she said, people often mistook them for husband and wife.

Her brother married, and Irma didn't like his wife. She never understood him, she said. They were not happy as a couple. They had three children who were always arguing and never took much notice of their father. Political turmoil in the area where they lived forced the family to move to another city, but he couldn't get the same kind of job, and hated the new one. He disliked the new city; he missed the contact with his brother and sisters and parents. It was three years now that they had been living there, but he had never settled. He was bitter about the enforced move and said it had ruined his career and his life. Then he developed a brain tumour, which caused a stroke. The doctors said he was dying; he couldn't be cured.

Irma was using up all her money on trips to Pakistan, spending as much time with him as she could. She detailed the conversations they had, the hours she spent with him exchanging childhood memories, the exercises she was doing for him, to loosen the paralysis.

All this was one-to-one with her brother, in his room. His wife and children were not included. And her own husband and children were in England, while she was away for a month or more at a time. Then she would come home, work to earn more money, and pay for another trip to Pakistan.

I asked about the effect on her husband and children. Her husband didn't count, she said; although they lived in the same house, they were separated now: just good friends. So he led his own life and it didn't make any difference if she was absent.

Her husband was sitting beside her while she said this, holding her hand and stroking it when she got too agitated. His eyes never left her face for the three hours that she talked.

And her children – well, they must just manage the best way they could, she said. They were old enough to cope. Besides, what could she do? Her brother needed her.

She would do anything – *anything* – she said, to save her brother. She must find someone, no matter what it cost, who had some gift who could save him.

When she stopped talking and waited, I said, 'I think you know your brother is going to die.'

Her eyes filled with tears and she said fiercely, 'He can't. He mustn't.'

'He has a reduced will to live, from the sound of it. He's lost his family life, his job, his home, his familiar surroundings, his social life. You say his wife is not patient with him and his children aren't close to him. What does he have to live for, in his own eyes?'

'He has me.'

'But you have to be here, with your children. And your husband, who still loves you.'

Her husband wouldn't meet her eyes when she looked at him, but he nodded.

'I don't care about them!' she said. 'Not like I care for my brother!'

'Perhaps that's what we should pray for, then. Would you like to?'

'You won't pray for him to be saved?'

'If you like, yes. But you might not agree with his way of saving himself, and God will give him first choice in what happens to him. Are you sure you wouldn't be praying against what he really wants for himself? Has he said what he wants? Did you ask him?'

Almost inaudibly, she said, 'He says he doesn't want to live.'

'Can you accept that?'

'No, never!'

'Can you accept that he does have a choice, and that God will respect it?'

'No! You have the wrong ideas. You're a Christian. Perhaps if I went to a Muslim...'

'Would it make any difference to what your brother wanted?'

She shook her head. 'No. No.'

'Irma, shall we pray for him to go in peace? Let him go gently?'

'If he dies I will kill myself!' she said.

'Then you wouldn't go in peace. Can we pray for your brother to die peacefully, knowing you don't blame him? And for you to go peacefully when your time comes, and then you'll be together. But only if you do it God's way. In the meantime, your own family need you. They wouldn't have any peace or joy again if you killed yourself. How about it?'

She looked through her tears at her husband who was also crying, with his head down, not looking at her, and something in her eyes softened.

'OK,' she said finally.

Sometimes, far from wanting to die, a person who has apparently nothing at all left to live for hangs on to life with astonishing persistence.

Gregory was a homeless alcoholic in his late thirties. He had been rejected by his family in early adulthood and had drifted into a lifestyle of drinking and spending his time with older homeless people on the street. By the time he was housed, he was unemployable.

His flat became a hang-out for other drinkers, and one night there was a fire. Nobody knew how it happened. Gregory was on his own there at the time. Someone eventually called the fire brigade, but Gregory's clothes had ignited and he had major burns over his entire body.

He was taken into intensive care, and wasn't expected to live for more than a few hours. But a week later, although he had to have artificial help in breathing, he was still alive.

Sister Bernadette, a nun who had known Gregory through a homeless centre he attended from time to time, was praying for him, and wondered if he was hanging on for some reason. With such bad burns she felt he could never recover, and the fact that he was surviving made her think he might have some unfinished business in this life. Bernadette was going up to the hospital to pray with him, and asked me if I wanted to come with her.

Gregory was in a separate room in the unit. Anyone who went in had to wear protective clothing because he was so exposed to infection. As soon as we went in, I saw why. He had no skin.

The bed was surrounded by cool air fans, which circulated the air around his burnt body – and circulated the stench. It was hard to believe someone could be so damaged and not be dead.

Gregory still had a face, but only just – that is, it was possible to see where the nose and mouth were, but there was no way of telling what he had looked like before the accident.

We went near, and Sister Bernadette told him we were here and who we were, and that we were going to pray with him. He kept trying to sit up, raising his red raw head and stretching out his arms. Every part of him was a wound, and every wound was oozing. The sight was terrible. And terrifying.

'Lord, you've got to help me,' I prayed. 'I'm going to be sick or faint. Take away my fear.'

'Whose fear?' came the response, very quietly.

It was true. The fear was in the room. It was pounding out of Gregory like the heat that was radiating from him. He was scared. And no wonder.

'Gregory, we know you're scared,' I said. 'But there's nothing you have to do. Just lie back and let everybody look after you. And we're going to pray now – OK? We'll pray for your fear to go.'

We prayed, and he went peaceful for a moment, but then started rearing up again, stretching his arms towards us.

The horrible thought came to me that he wanted to be held. He wanted the reassurance of human touch. But he was raw, and suppurating.

'Can he be touched?' I asked the nurse.

'No. Only with the gloves on. Don't remove your gloves.'

'I mean, does it hurt him?'

'Yes, we can't avoid that, I'm afraid. We're as careful as we can be.'

'Why does he keep sitting up?' Bernadette asked her. 'Is he in pain?'

He was letting out noises now, half-human sounds like a wounded animal.

'No, he's on very strong pain control,' the nurse said. 'He can't be in any pain.'

'Would you know if he was?' Bernadette asked.

'Yes, there are ways of telling.'

'I'm a nurse myself,' said Bernadette, 'but I haven't nursed in hospitals for twenty years. I'm not familiar with all the equipment you have here.'

'Give me a minute, then I'll show you everything,' the nurse promised.

She went out, and Bernadette said, 'I'm sure he's in pain.'

'Maybe it's spiritual pain,' I said.

'It could be. He could be afraid of dying. Or of not knowing what will happen when he does.'

She started to tell him that Jesus loved him and would take him home when the time came, but the nurse came back into the room and called her out for a few words.

I hadn't thought that I'd be left alone with Gregory, because there had been several nurses around him since we arrived, but suddenly I was – though I didn't know for how long. I had better make the most of it.

I stood at the foot of the bed and said, 'Gregory, listen. God knows you, and if there's anything you've done in your life that you're worried about, he is telling you now that you're forgiven. You've suffered enough. Now I can't understand you when you talk, so I want you just to tell God if you're worried about anything. Then I'll ask him if there's anything he wants to say to you. All right?'

He sat completely still for a moment, half-raised from the bed, and seemed to be listening. I didn't know if he could hear me or not, but it had to be worth a try.

'Father,' I said aloud. 'This is Gregory. He's your son. If you're going to take him home soon, is there anything you want to say to him now?'

Gregory was still half-sitting up, his eyeless face turned towards me.

There were sounds outside the room. 'Hurry up, Lord,' I prayed silently. Then I heard him clearly.

'Gregory, Jesus wants to say this to you,' I said, loudly and quickly. 'He says, "Today you will be with me in paradise." Got that? Good. And I want to tell you I love you, Gregory, and I'll see you again later on. But, "Today you will be with me in paradise." Right?'

The door opened and two nurses came in. They made Gregory lie down and started checking his monitors. Sister Bernadette came back. The room was suddenly busy.

'Have you finished praying?' she asked.

'Yes. Have you?'

'Yes. I think so.'

'Do you think he's going to survive?' she asked, as we were making our way out of the building.

I told her what I had heard.

'That's great!' she said. 'He's going to die today then!'

'I don't know if it means today, literally. I took it to mean he's with God now and the minute he dies he'll be with him for eternity. No gap.'

'It could be.' She quoted the Bible: 'With the Lord, a day is like a thousand years, and a thousand years is like a day.' Then she said soberly, 'It won't be long, anyway. The nurse told me that as soon as the family arrive, they'll be taking Gregory off the ventilator. He'll die then, immediately.'

Over the next few days, the family came. Permission was given to switch off the life-support system, and Gregory was moved to another room, to a normal bed, with no equipment. The relatives were there, and began talking to one another – something that some of them hadn't done for years. Only one uncle was missing. There was no way they could get in touch with him straight away, and then no way he could get there, for two weeks. And Gregory now had no ventilator. But he started to breathe, unaided.

He lived for fourteen days, in that room where he had been put to die. And finally, after the uncle's visit and his reconciliation with the rest of the family, Gregory stopped breathing.

I look forward to meeting him, when the time comes. Sister Bernadette said he had a nice face.

21

I know there are far more miracles going on than we get to hear about. I know because I hear about some of them, but generally only when I've been in conversation with someone for a while and they feel confident that I believe in the reality of God's power achieving the impossible.

People who have received or witnessed miracles are generally reticent about them. What they can't keep quiet about is God, and how great he is. But the details of what they have seen him do are so treasured and so personal, that to open them up to debate among the cynical is not an option they relish. They know, in advance, what a cynic would do with a miracle. Deny it.

Some of the lengths people go to, in explaining away something unexplainable that has occurred in response to prayer, are ridiculous! The explanations they come up with are far more unlikely than the simple event of God's intervention in his own creation, at a moment of his own choosing.

I saw a television programme the other night. A man had had the same dream ten nights in succession, about a plane crashing. Every detail of it was clear. On the eleventh night, a plane crashed – in the way he had dreamed it would happen, in the same place, with all the details exactly accurate.

A psychologist was interviewed, and said that the dream was a projection of something within himself, its repetition meant it was important to him, and the timing and details of the crash were coincidences.

While I'm not keen on being bombarded with 'amazing supernatural' interpretations of only very slightly unusual happenings, some coincidences are just too coincidental to be accidental. So, we don't have an explanation of why the man had that dream. Nor did he, but he wasn't trying to explain it. He was honest about what had happened to him, and honest in saying he didn't understand it.

I have occasionally had images of things about to happen. It can be quite disturbing, and I don't think anyone would willingly imagine such things. To see what can't be seen yet, physically, may be a gift but it's not an easy one to receive. If it is a gift from God, then all his gifts have a purpose. And the purpose of any of his spiritual gifts is not for the benefit of the person who has the gift, but for the people God wants to help by means of it.

I doubt very much that if that man had contacted the airline staff and warned them that a crash was forthcoming they would have done anything more than laugh about him during their coffee break.

On the rare occasions that I've received a similar warning of what could happen, the purpose of it has been to pray. It's a vision of what is going to happen *if events continue along the course they are currently taking*. What we're called to do is to pray that that course of events will change.

At one time, night after night when I was praying I saw a horrifying scene of a woman I knew being beaten up viciously by her husband. I could see it, hear it, and feel it as if it were real. I kept trying to stop him hitting her, and praying to God to stop him, but it didn't happen. He seemed completely out of control. There was no way of stopping him.

The scene was getting worse each night – or at least, I was seeing more of it. The children coming in and screaming. The grandmother calling an ambulance, and trying to make her son leave his wife alone.

If I don't get an answer to prayer fairly swiftly, I usually go back to the drawing board and check that I'm praying for the right thing. If the prayer needs to change, I ask the Lord to show me. On this occasion, my prayer for the man to stop taking out his violence on his wife was not having any effect. So I changed the prayer and prayed that I would be allowed to get between them and he would hit me instead, and she would be free to comfort the children and get them away from the scene of violence. They were aged four and three.

The next night, the same vision occurred, only this time he hit me instead of his wife. I felt it. It seemed completely real to me: the fear, and the pain. He beat me unconscious and, in reality, I didn't wake up till next morning, feeling very much the worse for wear.

The following night, the scene recurred in the same way and I prayed again – for whatever the solution to this pattern of violence was. I was 'beaten up' again. And the next night, and the one afterwards.

That last time, the violence didn't seem to last so long, and I started talking to him, and he started calming down. I told him he had to leave his wife alone, or he would have God to reckon with – and the Father can deal with people with a very firm hand.

He said he was afraid of attacking his children. That was his real fear. They were so small and vulnerable, and he could feel his anger rising so high at times that he feared they weren't safe. He had no grudge really against his wife, or me, but he had to take it out on someone. If he didn't hit somebody adult, he was so afraid his anger would flare with the kids over some small thing and he wouldn't be able to control it, and he would hurt them – even kill them. He would never forgive himself if he caused them harm, because he loved them. He just couldn't escape his own violence.

I told him I would pray, and he wouldn't be allowed to hurt his children. God would intervene.

The next night, I no longer saw this scene when I prayed.

It was about a month later that I was visiting this same family. It was in the evening and the children had just gone to bed. I went up to say goodnight to them and they clamoured for a story. So they both climbed into one bed and I sat beside them and started to read.

I heard their father come upstairs and there was a noise on the landing – something scraping against the wall. He came in with an old replica gun that they had on the wall as an ornament, knelt down by his children's bed, and slammed the gun down hard on the bed, between me and the children.

A symbol of violence. And of his fear of how he might use it?

I smiled at him and carried on reading. The children, who had jumped, relaxed again. After a tense moment, he sat back on his heels and listened. I picked up another book and went straight into it as soon as we got to the end of the last story, and the four of us sat there, hearing about bunnies and the smiley moon in the sky, and other safe images of childhood.

After a while he got up, took the gun and hung it back on the wall, and went downstairs.

His wife told me, a few years later, that her husband used to hit her, but that he had stopped. He had stopped watching the violent videos he used to like too.

I asked her if he had ever hit the children, and she said no. Never. 'He's not that kind of person. He wouldn't do that, however angry he was.'

How much of what we see 'in the mind's eye', or in spirit during times of prayer, is real? How much of it is creative imagination? Or something else? I don't know. But when it seems too uncomfortably close to reality, it may be more dangerous to dismiss it out of fear of being silly than to assume it might be correct and act on it. And the action that's appropriate is to pray. Prayer changes things.

In the past couple of years, some people who have been present at or involved in miracles have told me about them. A woman had a heart attack during a healing service; an ambulance was called, but two nurses who were at the service pronounced her already dead; there was no sign of life, no breath, no pulse, and she had turned yellow.

The priest asked for her to be taken into the sacristy, prayed over her, breathed over her, and told her to open her eyes. She opened them. And at her next hospital check it was found that her heart condition was no longer a problem.

I sat next to a woman at a day retreat. She told me her prayer group had been praying for her daughter's music teacher, who had only three months to live. Her breathing was so bad she couldn't get up from the chair without becoming breathless. The members of the group had prayed and fasted for her, over a period of a couple of months – right up until the expected time of her death.

Now, eighteen months later, she was too busy to take on more music pupils. After her healing she had become a fitness enthusiast, and went jogging and to the gym three times a week. She had just finished training to become an aerobics instructor.

I believed both of these accounts: the first one because it was told me by Father Adam, who was there. The second one was told to me with extreme hesitation, after the lady had made some rather cryptic comments about how good God is and how worthwhile it is to persevere in prayer, against all the odds.

I have heard of some other happenings that I don't know whether to believe or not. All I do know is, when I'm listening to them I feel I don't want to hear any more – which is odd because it normally feels like an enormous privilege to hear anything about the current activities of God.

I know I never, ever, want to see another set of blurry photographs from some part of the world where the Virgin Mary is meant to be appearing, and be told that that blob in the background is unmistakably her. Nor an ever-so-slightly computer-enhanced image of her face. None of these 'real, live, unique and genuine' pictures of her resemble each other at all. And they all look like statues, whereas none of the people I know who have seen her in spirit say she is anything like the tall, statuesque, rather Hollywood image these pictures portray.

That the mother of Jesus chooses to appear to

people, I have no hesitation in accepting. There is nothing surprising in a mother choosing to speak to her own adopted children, especially at times when they may be in trouble or at risk. And of course she has the right to speak to her children in any way God wishes – wherever, whenever and however may be most effective.

But the efforts of some people to convince everybody they meet that a miracle has occurred, and their insistence on their 'proof' being accepted, suggest to me that they are not convinced themselves. When someone is sure that God has done something special in their life, they may keep quiet about it for years – for ever, in some cases. When they do talk about it, it's for a purpose: so that people with faith will be encouraged to go on praying and know that it never fails to have an effect.

Let anyone who is able to accept that miracles occur, accept it. Let anyone who can't, hold on to their own opinions. Miracles are not for cynics – or not for those cynics determined to stay cynical. God will give them their own signs, in their own time.

Private miracles occur all the time, in the lives of very different people, and most of them stay private. When they are shared, it's a privilege. When they are dissected, over-explained, or ridiculed, it's a shame. But it doesn't affect the truth.

God doesn't always act in ways we accept as normal. His idea of normal is not always the same.

His idea of love is not the same as ours either, or not always: it's far wider, more encompassing, and some-times more painful and demanding.

He doesn't shy away from distressing short-term suffering as a remedy for world-scale, long-term problems.

He doesn't seem frightened of death or tragedy. His

involvement in it is what makes sense of the senseless disasters in the world. And brings even death to life with a purpose.

What's wrong with God?

Why doesn't he do things our way?

Maybe he is the only one who does.